D1030404

WITHDRAWN

When euer ye Natiues haue
desir'd Satisfaction, (as
knowing yt we haue inclded
ye Bounds set vs by ye Sa-
chims) we haue Satisfied them.

Roger Wjlljams.

THE

EARLY HISTORY

OF

Rhode-Island.

AN

HISTORICAL DISCOURSE,

ON

THE CIVIL AND RELIGIOUS AFFAIRS

OF THE COLONY OF

RHODE-ISLAND.

BY JOHN CALLENDER

WITH A MEMOIR OF THE AUTHOR; BIOGRAPHICAL NOTICES OF
SOME OF HIS DISTINGUISHED CONTEMPORARIES;

AND ANNOTATIONS AND ORIGINAL DOCUMENTS ILLUSTRATIVE OF
THE HISTORY OF RHODE-ISLAND AND PROVIDENCE PLAN-
TATIONS, FROM THE FIRST SETTLEMENT TO THE
END OF THE FIRST CENTURY.

BY ROMEO ELTON

———

Nescire quid antea quam natus sis acciderit, id est semper esse puerum.
CICERO

———

THIRD EDITION.

———

 BOOKS FOR LIBRARIES PRESS
FREEPORT, NEW YORK

CALVIN T. RYAN LIBRARY
KEARNEY STATE COLLEGE
KEARNEY, NEBRASKA

First Published 1843
Reprinted 1971

INTERNATIONAL STANDARD BOOK NUMBER:
0-8369-5685-0

LIBRARY OF CONGRESS CATALOG CARD NUMBER:
79-150172

PRINTED IN THE UNITED STATES OF AMERICA

CONTENTS.

ADVERTISEMENT.

In 1836, the Editor was appointed by the R. I. Historical Society, to revise Callender's Century Discourse for republication, and to prepare a biographical sketch of the author, &c. When ready for the press, in accordance with the practice of the Trustees, a Committee was appointed to make a report to the Board, and the work was published as Vol. 4, of the Society's Collections. It is thought proper, therefore, to retain the Preface. As no portrait of the venerable Roger Williams exists, as the best substitute, a fac-simile of his autograph is prefixed to this edition.

The encouraging approbation bestowed on this work by the public, and the favorable notice which it has received from the leading Reviews, Literary and Religious, in the various sections of the Union, are gratifying to the Editor, as indicating an increasing interest in those studies and researches which relate to the history of our country.

ROMEO ELTON.

Brown University, March, 1843.

PREFACE.

It has, for several years, been the desire and intention of the Rhode-Island Historical Society to cause Callender's Historical Discourse, with appropriate notes and a selection of documents requisite for its illustration, to be embodied in their published Collections. The original edition of the Discourse, which was published in 1739, has long been out of print. Of that edition but few copies remain perfect, and even these are extremely rare. The propriety, and indeed necessity, of its republication has been rendered greater during each succeeding year, by the increased attention which has been paid to the early history of New-England, among the memorials of which, this work has ever been held in high and merited estimation.

In the accomplishment of this object, it has been fortunate for the Society that the editorship of the present edition, with the task of preparing such notes and additions as it was desirable should accompany it, has been undertaken by one qualified to discharge it with so much ability. The original materials which Professor Elton has contributed, the information contained in the notes, respecting distinguished individuals whose names are connected with the history of the Colony during the first century, add much to the value of the work; and when it is considered how little has been known in rela-

tion to the life of Mr. Callender, we feel confident
that every reader of the Discourse will be gratified
to find so interesting a Memoir of its author.

The Appendix of historical documents is extensive and well selected. All the papers which it
contains, not only deserve a place in the Collections
of the Society, but are also particularly valuable as
explanatory of the facts narrated in the Discourse,
conveying, as they do, full information on many
points to which brief references only could be made
in a work written for such an occasion. With regard to the manner in which these documents are
here published, the Committee are happy in bearing
testimony to the unwearied care and minute exam-
ination which have been bestowed in their prepara-
tion for the press. In every instance, they have
been carefully compared with the originals, and no
pains have been spared to ensure their correctness.

In presenting this volume, the Committee can
therefore speak with much confidence respecting
the manner in which Professor Elton has met the
wishes of the Historical Society. He is entitled to
the thanks of that Society, for the valuable addition
which he has made to their Collections, and deserves
the grateful remembrance of the people of our State,
for the satisfactory manner in which he has illustra-
ted this history of their forefathers.

ALBERT G. GREENE,
WILLIAM G. GODDARD.
Providence, April, 1838.

MEMOIR

OF THE

REV. JOHN CALLENDER, A. M.

BIOGRAPHY, as well as history, is too frequently employed in eulogizing men who have distinguished themselves merely as crafty statesmen or as ambitious warriors. The historian and the biographer say little of those characters who are actuated by christian principle, and who seek not *the praise of men, but of God.* Moral excellence, however, is the most beneficial to mankind; and it is but justice to allow it to participate in those honors which are more usually appropriated to men of great depravity of heart, and who employ their fellow men only as tools for advancing their own ambition. The biography of a person of unostentatious piety and goodness, may afford more useful instruction to the majority of readers, than the dazzling exploits of an Alexander the Great, a Julius Cæsar, or a Buonaparte.

The subject of the following memoir, died nearly a century ago, and it is to be regretted that the materials to fill up his character are not more ample; particularly those parts of his private conduct, which would have made us familiar with this excellent man, and imparted a graphic reality to the portrait. The imperfect sketch which follows, will not do justice to the subject, but it may, at least, furnish a few facts respecting a man who possessed a mind of no ordinary vigor, and whose memory is still precious.

The Rev. JOHN CALLENDER was born of reputable parents, in the city of Boston, Mass., A. D. 1706. His father, John Callender, Esq., was the son of the Rev. Ellis Callender, the highly honored and esteemed minister of the first Baptist Church in Boston from 1708 till 1726. Elisha Callender, his son, uncle to the subject of this memoir, became his successor in the pastoral office. This gentleman was educated at Harvard College, and was one of the fourteen students who were graduated in the year 1710. At his ordination, which took place May 21, 1718, three Congregational ministers gave their assistance, viz. Dr. Increase Mather, Dr. Cotton Mather, and Rev. John Webb. Dr. Cotton Mather preached the ordination sermon, which was entitled, *Good Men United.**

This expression of Christian feeling on the part of the Congregational ministers in Boston, and the catholic spirit which existed at Cambridge, induced Thomas Hollis, Esq. of London, a wealthy merchant, of the Baptist denomination, to bestow

* See note A.

very large benefactions upon Harvard College. Besides making large additions to its library and philosophical apparatus, he founded two professorships in that Institution, one of Divinity, and one of Mathematics and Natural Philosophy, and endowed the College to the amount of a hundred pounds a year, to be distributed among ten scholars of good character.*

Mr. Callender continued faithful and successful in the pastoral office, till his death, March 31, 1738. A few days before he died, he said, " When I look on one hand, I see nothing but sin, guilt and discouragement; but when I look on the other, I see my glorious Saviour, and the merits of his precious blood which cleanseth from all sin. I cannot say, I have such transports of joy as some have had, but through grace I can say, I have gotten the victory over death and the grave." His obituary in the public newspaper, three days after his death, was in the following words: "On Friday morning last, after a lingering sickness, deceased the Rev. Mr. Elisha Callender, minister of the Baptist Church in this town; a gentleman universally beloved by people of all persuasions for his charitable and catholic way of thinking. His life was unspotted, and his conversation always affable, religious, and truly manly. During his long illness, he was remarkably patient, and, in his last hours, like the blessed above, pacific and entirely serene; his

* See note B.

senses were good to the last. 'I shall,' said he,
'sleep in Jesus,' and that moment expired, very
much lamented by all that knew him." He published a century sermon in the year 1720, com-
memorative of the landing of our forefathers at
Plymouth, which has furnished important information for succeeding historians.

Of the early years of JOHN CALLENDER, the subject of the following narrative, we have little information. At the age of thirteen he entered Harvard
College, where he received the benefit of Mr. Hollis's
donation. The Hon. John Leverett, F. R. S. was
at that time its President, a man whose mental
excellencies were adorned by the noblest moral
qualities. Here, his vigorous understanding was
cultivated, a proper direction given to his activity,
and his mind imbued with the principles of virtue
and religion. He graduated from that Institution in
1723. In the same year, he was baptised on a profession of faith, and united with the first Baptist
Church in Boston, of which his uncle was pastor.
He was licensed to preach by this church, in June,
1727. In August, 1728, he received and accepted
an invitation from the Baptist Church in Swansey,
the oldest in Massachusetts, to supply their pulpit,
and continued laboring among this people until
February 15, 1730. Soon after, he received a request from the first Baptist Church in Newport, to
visit and preach to them. This was the second
Baptist Church in America, and was founded in

1644. After long and mature deliberation and earnest prayer, he accepted the invitation of that Church to the pastoral office, and was ordained, October 13, 1731. Rev. Elisha Callender, of Bos- ton, preached on the occasion, from Matthew xxviii; 18, 19. Mr. Callender continued the faithful and beloved pastor of this church and congregation, till he was called to his final rest.

Soon after his settlement in Newport, he became a member of a literary and philosophical society es- tablished in that place. The celebrated Dean, afterwards Bishop Berkeley, who resided there at that time, is thought to have suggested its forma- tion.* The society was select, and some of its members were men of great intellectual power— among whom were Judge Edward Scott, Hon. Daniel Updike, Governor Josias Lyndon, Dr. John Brett, Hon. Thomas Ward, Hon. William Ellery, Rev. James Honyman, Rev. James Searing, Rev. John Checkley, jun., and Rev. Jeremiah Condy, of Boston. Among the occasional members were Governor Stephen Hopkins and Samuel Johnson, D. D., afterwards President of Columbia College, New-York. As this was probably one of the earliest societies of the kind in this country, we have thought proper to subjoin a copy of its rules and regulations, the original of which, (in the hand writing of Judge Scott,) is in the archives of the Rhode-Island Historical Society.

* See note C.

"Whereas, A. D. 1730, Messrs. Daniel Updike, Peter Bours, James Searing, Edward Scott, Henry Collins, Nathan Townsend, Jeremiah Condy and James Honeyman, jun. did form a Society for the promotion of Knowledge and Virtue, by a free conversation according to several regulations by them agreed.

"We the present members of the said Society, finding it necessary on many accounts for the more effectual answering the end of our Institution, do agree to enter into a more strict engagement, and establish the following as the laws and orders to be observed in this Society.

" 1   The members of the Society shall meet every Monday evening, at the house of one of the members, *seriatim*, and converse about and debate, some useful question in Divinity, Morality, Philosophy History, &c.

"2. The member who proposed the question, shall be moderator, (*pro hac vice*) and see that order and decency be maintained in all the debates and conversation.

" 3. Every member in order shall freely give his opinion with his reasons, having liberty to explain the sense of the question, or his own expressions, and to retract or alter his opinion as to him shall seem right.

" 4. The member at whose house we meet shall propose a question for the next evening's conversation, the Society to judge of its propriety and usefulness, only nothing shall ever be proposed or debated which is a distinguishing religious tenet of any one member.

" 5. No member shall divulge the opinion or arguments of any particular member as to any subject debated in the Society, on penalty of a perpetual exclusion. Nevertheless, any member may gratify the curiosity of any that may inquire the names, number, general design, method and laws of the Society, and the opinions or conclusions of the major part, without discovering how any particular member voted.

" 6. The moderator for the time being shall keep a book, in which he shall register the questions and the solutions or answers, and another for the fines and forfeits that may become due.

"7. The question shall be propounded by the moderator exactly at seven in the evening, or if he be then absent another shall be chosen in his room, and whoever shall come after that, shall forfeit one shilling; whoever is absent the whole evening, shall forfeit two shillings and six pence; only the moderator shall forfeit double. Whoever shall make it an excuse to avoid giving his opinion, that he has not thought of the question, or has forgot what the question is, shall forfeit one shilling. Whoever is unprovided of a proper question, on his turn to propound it, shall forfeit one shilling. He that omits to register the question or solution in his turn, shall forfeit two shillings and six pence. A treasurer shall be chosen once in three months, and whoever shall refuse an office when chosen, shall forfeit five shillings. And every treasurer that is deficient in his duty in collecting the fines, shall pay them himself. No excuse shall be taken for absence but sickness in person, or family, or the being out of town. The fines shall be gathered every month, and be laid out in books, &c., as the Society shall think best. Whoever shall absent himself a quarter of a year successively, without sufficient excuse, shall have his name struck out of the list.

"8. Any member may bring with him any friend or stranger who shall desire it, and whom he may think may not be offensive to any other member.

"9. Any member may propose a candidate, but none shall be admitted without the full and free consent of every member, to be manifested in written votes, after a month's probation. However, the same person that has been negatived, may be propounded again by another member.

"10. If the Society incline to choose any gentlemen at a distance to be occasional members, their election shall be made in the same manner; they shall be subject to the same rules of secrecy, and have the same liberty to speak and debate any subject with the other members, and shall vote in all occasional matters.

" 11. The laws shall be publicly read in the Society every three months, on the same evening that the treasurer is chosen. And every member shall then produce his copy, upon the forfeiture of two shillings and six pence.

" 12. Every member shall promote the good of the Society, as far as lies in his power.

" 13. Each of the present members shall sign these articles in the book, and shall have a copy of them, signed by the moderator for the time being, to be and remain as a proof and token of our fellowship and society. And every gentleman that may hereafter be chosen a member, shall enter his name in the same manner, and have a copy of the laws signed as above, together with a list of the Society, and a copy of the additional or explanatory laws that may hereafter be made.

Newport, February 2, 1735.

DANIEL UPDIKE,	JOHN BRETT,
PETER BOURS,	CHARLES BARDIN,
EDWARD SCOTT,	J. HONYMAN, jun. Feb. 9th.
NATHAN TOWNSEND,	HEZ. CARPENTER, May 24, 1736
SAMUEL WICKHAM,	JAMES SEARING,

THOMAS WARD,   JOSEPH JACOB,
JOSIAS LYNDON,   WILLIAM ELLERY, Oct. 3, 1737
JOHN CALLENDER, jun.   JOS. SYLVESTER,
SUETON GRANT,   JOHN CHECKLEY, jun.

OCCASIONAL MEMBERS.

JOHN ADAMS,   JOHN WALLACE,
DANIEL HUBBARD,   STEPHEN HOPKINS,
JEREMIAH CONDY,   SAMUEL JOHNSON.

" Oct. 3, 1737. Voted, That every member who shall neglect to bring or send the book of fines, shall forfeit two shillings and six pence. A true copy, compared with the Society's book, by

EDWARD SCOTT, Moderator."

One of the objects of this Society was the collection of valuable books. It was subsequently joined by Abraham Redwood, Esq. who gave the the sum of five hundred pounds sterling to increase its library, on condition the Society would build a suitable edifice. The Society obtained a charter from the Colony in 1747, by the name of The Company of the Redwood Library. In 1748, the present classical building was erected, from a design by Harrison, the assistant architect of Blenheim House, England. This library contains many choice and rare European editions.

Apart from his more ordinary employment and influence as a minister of the gospel, Mr. Callender acted an important part in relation to the more general and public interests of the town and State.

In civil matters he was much consulted, and frequent and honorable mention of his name appears on the records of the town. His character commanded the respect and confidence not only of his own church and society, but also of the State of which he was an intelligent and useful citizen.

In 1739, Mr. Callender published a historical discourse on the civil and religious affairs of the Colony of Rhode-Island, from the settlement in 1638 to the end of the first century, usually known by the name of the "Century Sermon." This is the only history of the Colony or State of Rhode Island, which has been written, and though small, it is a noble and enduring monument to the talent and piety of its author. It is written with great fidelity, is distinguished by solid and profound philosophical views, and by an ardent attachment to the principles of civil and religious freedom. It breathes a spirit of candor, impartiality, and enlightened piety, in ever page. Mr. Callender evidently took great pains in investigating the sources from which he drew his information, and his observations on men and things indicate an acute, observant and reflecting mind.

In the same year, he published a sermon preached at the ordination of Mr. Jeremiah Condy, A. M., to the pastoral care of the Baptist Church in Boston. In this sermon, the liberal sentiments of Mr. Callender on the subject of free communion, are fully exhibited. After earnestly inculcating the duty of all Christians loving one another as brethren, he observes, " But I have trespassed too much upon your patience already, and shall therefore only beg leave to add, that if that *glorious principle* which was a fundamental article in the constitution of the first *Baptist Church*, gathered in this *Province*, could be fully acted upon, we might with the utmost propriety, join the heavenly host, and sing, *Glory to God in the highest : Peace on earth, and good will towards and among men.* For they *declared* in their *church covenant*, " *That union to Christ was the sole ground of their communion with each other*, and that they were ready to *accept of, receive to, and hold church-communion with, all such, as in a judgment of charity, were fellow-members with them in their head Christ Jesus, though differing in such controversial points, as are not absolutely and essentially necessary to salvation.*"*

The religious sentiments of Mr. Callender were ever thus fearlessly avowed and honestly maintained. His inflexible integrity did not permit him to conceal the convictions of his mind on any subject which he thought affected the social, political or moral interests of mankind.

Mr. Callender was ingenious in devising plans of usefulness, and especially in endeavoring to promote the welfare of the young. In 1741, he pub-

* See note D.

lished a sermon on the advantages of early religion, preached to a society of young men in Newport. This sermon is replete with sound practical instruction, flowing from a heart warmed with the love of God.

In the year 1745, Mr. Callender published a discourse occasioned by the death of his friend, the Rev. Mr. Clap, in which he pays a tribute of affectionate veneration to his memory. Mr. Callender's sermon was founded on Hebrews xiii. 7, 8.

The prominent traits in the character of Mr. Clap, are faithfully delineated in the following extracts from that sermon :

" The main stroke in his character was his eminent sanctity and piety, and an ardent desire to promote the knowledge and practice of true godliness in others. As his understanding was above the common level, so was his learning, though he studiously concealed it. He thought his station required more than common instances of innocency, self-denial and caution.

" He was zealously attached to what he considered as the true doctrines of grace, and to the forms of worship he thought to be of divine institution. But his charity embraced good men of all denominations. He had little value for mere speculative, local, nominal christianity, and a form of godliness without the power. He insisted most on those things on which our interest in Jesus Christ and our title to eternal life must depend: that *faith* by which we are justified and have peace with God through our Lord Jesus, and that *repentance* towards God and *new obedience,* which are the necessary effect and evidence of our regeneration, and the proper exercise of christianity.

" He abounded in contrivances to do good by scattering books of piety and virtue, not such as minister questions and strife, but godly edifying, and put himself to a very considerable expense, that he might, in this method, awaken the careless and secure, comfort the feeble minded, succor the tempted, instruct the ignorant, and quicken, animate and encourage all.

"He abounded in acts of charity to the poor and necessitous—to whom he was a kind father and guardian.

" In fine, he was a public blessing, as an able minister of the New Testament, an example of unsuspected piety, and an honor to religion.

" There are two things in which he excelled in so remarkable a manner, that 1 must not omit them : his care about the education of children, and his concern for the instruction of servants.

" The conclusion of his life and ministry was a peaceful and happy death, without those raptures which some boast of, but with perfect resignation to the will of God, and good hope and humble confidence in Christ Jesus, who was the sum of his doctrine and the end of his conversation."*

* See Note E.

Mr. Callender collected many papers relating to the history of the Baptist denomination in this country, which were used by the Rev. Isaac Backus in his Church History of New-England.

After a long and painful illness, which he bore with Christian resignation, he died in full expectation of the blessedness of the righteous, January 26, 1748, in the 42d year of his age.

Mr. Callender, on the 15th of February, 1730, was married to Elizabeth Hardin, of Swansey, Mass. By this lady he had six children : Elizabeth, Mary, John, Elias, Sarah and Josias. The following description of his person is taken principally from an original portrait : He was about the middle size, graceful and well proportioned. His complexion was fair, his features were regular, his forehead was high and prominent, and in his countenance there was an admirable mixture of gravity and sweetness. His eyes were of a dark blue, and said to be remarkable for their intelligence and brilliancy.

The character of Mr. Callender, both in public and private life, was truly amiable and excellent. Whether viewed as a citizen, a relative, a friend, a christian, or a minister of the gospel, he adorned the sphere in which he moved.

His remains were interred in the common bury-
ing ground at Newport, where a tomb was erected
to his memory, on which is the following inscription,
composed by Dr. Moffatt, a celebrated physician
of that town:

"Confident of awaking, here reposeth
JOHN CALLENDER;
Of very excellent endowments from nature,
And of an accomplished education,
Improved by application in the wide circle
Of the more polite arts and useful sciences.
From motives of conscience and grace
He dedicated himself to the immediate service
Of God,
In which he was distinguished as a shining
And very burning light by a true and faithful
Ministry of seventeen years in the first Baptist
Church of Rhode-Island; where the purity
And evangelical simplicity of his doctrine,confirmed
And embellished by the virtuous and devout tenor
Of his own life,
Endeared him to his flock, and justly conciliated
The esteem, love and reverence of all the
Wise, worthy and good.
Much humility, benevolence and charity
Breathed in his conversation, discourses and writ-
ings,

Which were all pertinent, reasonable and useful.
Regretted by all; lamented by his friends; and
Deeply deplored by a wife and numerous issue,
He died,
In the forty-second year of his age,
January 26, 1748;
Having struggled through the vale of life
In adversity, much sickness and pain,
With fortitude, dignity and elevation of soul,
Worthy of the Philosopher, Christian and Divine."

4

NOTES TO THE MEMOIR.

Note A—p. 10.

Dr. Cotton Mather, in his ordination sermon, after alluding to the severities which had been used against Christians by the ruling powers, says:

"Cursed the anger, for it is fierce, and the wrath, for it is cruel; good for nothing but only to make divisions in Jacob and dispersions in Israel. Good men, alas! good men have done such ill things as these; yea few churches of the reformation have been wholly clear of these iniquities. New-England, also, has in some former times done something of this aspect, which would not now be so well approved of; in which, if the brethren in whose house we are now convened, met with any thing too unbrotherly, they now with satisfaction hear us expressing our dislike of every thing which looked like persecution in the days that have passed over us."

The following is the copy of the letter sent to the Church under the care of Dr. Mather and Rev. Mr. Webb, on Mr. Callender's ordination:

" *Honored and beloved in the Lord,*

" Considering that there ought to be a holy fellowship maintained among godly Christians, and that it is a duty for us to receive one another as Christ also received us to the glory of God, notwithstanding some differing persuasions in matters of doubtful disputation; and although we have not so great latitude as to the subject of baptism as the churches of New-England generally have; notwithstanding, as to the fundamental principles in your doctrine of Christ, both as to the faith and order of the gospel, we concur with them; being also satisfied that particular churches have power from Christ to choose their own pastors, and that elders ought to be ordained in every Church; and having chosen our well beloved brother, Elisha Callender, to be our pastor, we entreat you to send your elders and messengers to give the Right Hand of Fellowship in his ordination."

Note B—p. 11.

Thomas Hollis, Esq., was a great patron and friend of learning. He was a Baptist, but not a sectarian. What he required in the character of the professor of divinity was, "that he should be a man of solid learning in divinity, of sound and orthodox principles, one who is well gifted to teach, of a sober and pious life, and of a grave conversation."*

The following extract is taken from a sermon delivered before the General Court, by Dr. Benjamin Colman, of Boston, occasioned by the death of Mr. Hollis:

" He was one of those righteous men who should be had in everlasting remembrance. Like *Araunah*, he gave

* Pierce's History of Harvard University, Ap. p. 96.

as a prince. Of his own mere motion he poured in upon us, and upon other places also, from time to time, as a living spring whose waters fail not. That which is *singular* in the piety and benefits of Mr. Hollis unto these churches was, that he was not strictly of our way, nor in judgment with us in point of infant baptism ; yet his heart and hand was the same to us, *as if we had been one* in opinion and practice with him. And in this let him stand a *teaching pattern* and example to us of a noble, Christian, and catholic spirit of love."

" It was some account he received from us of the free and catholic air we breathe at Cambridge, where protestants of every denomination may have their children educated, and graduated in our college, if they behave with sobriety and virtue, that took his generous heart and fixed it on us, and enlarged it to us. And this shall be with me among his distinguishing praises, while we rise up and bless his memory ; that is, bless God in remembrance of all the undeserved favors done us by him."—*Colman's Life.*

The first professor of divinity in Harvard College, was Rev. Edward Wigglesworth, D. D., chosen in 1721, at the age of thirty. He was a classmate of Rev. Elisha Callender, and occupied the divinity chair more than forty years, with a high reputation for piety and learning.

Note C.—p. 13.

*Biographical Sketch of Dean Berkeley, afterwards
Bishop of Cloyne, who resided on Rhode-Island,
1729—1731.*

Dr. GEORGE BERKELEY was born at Kilkrin, in
Ireland, in 1684. He was educated at Trinity
College, Dublin, where he distinguished himself by
his literary attainments and the superior powers
of his mind. He became a Fellow of Trinity
College in 1707; and was created D. D. in 1717.
By the recommendation of Swift, he accompanied,
as chaplain and secretary, the celebrated Earl of
Peterborough, who was appointed ambassador to
Sicily; and afterwards, when disappointed in his
expectations of preferment, he spent four years on
the Continent, as travelling tutor to the son of Dr.
Ashe, Bishop of Clogher. Shortly after his return
to London, in 1721, he was appointed chaplain to
the lord lieutenant of Ireland, the Duke of Grafton.
By a legacy of Miss Vanhomrigh, the Vanessa of
Swift, his fortune was considerably increased. In
1724, on being promoted to the Deanry of Derry,
he resigned his Fellowship. He now published his
proposals for the conversion of the American
savages to Christianity, by the establishment of a
College in the Bermuda Islands. The plan was
very favorably received; and he obtained a charter
for a College, in which he was named the first
President. He received, also, from Sir Robert
Walpole, a promise of a grant of twenty thousand

pounds to carry it into effect. Having resigned his living, worth eleven thousand pounds per annum, and all his hopes of preferment, he set sail for the field of his distant labors, with his family, and three Fellows of Trinity College, and several literary and scientfiic gentlemen. He landed at Newport, after a tedious passage of five months, January 23, 1729. His arrival is thus announced in the New-England Weekly Journal:

"NEWPORT, January 24, 1729.
" Yesterday arrived here, Dean Berkeley, of *London-derry*, in a pretty large ship. He is a gentleman of middle stature, of an agreeable, pleasant, and erect aspect. He was ushered into the town with a great number of gentlemen, to whom he behaved after a very complaisant manner. ' Tis said he purposes to tarry here with his family about three months."

The following extract of a letter was written by Dean Berkeley to Thomas Prior, Esq., of Dublin, soon after his arrival at Newport :

"NEWPORT, in Rhode-Island, April 24, 1729.
" I can by this time say something to you, from my own experience, of this place and people. The inhabitants are of a mixed kind, consisting of many sects and subdivisions of sects. Here are four sorts of Anabaptists, besides Presbyterians, Quakers, Independents, and many of no profession at all. Notwithstanding so many differences, here are fewer quarrels about religion than elsewhere, the people living peaceably with their neighbors of whatsoever

persuasion.   They all agree in one point, that the church
of England is the second best.   The climate is like that
of Italy, and not at all colder in the winter than I have
known it every where north of Rome.   The spring is
late ; but to make amends, they assure me the autumns
are the finest and longest in the world ; and the sum-
mers are much pleasanter than those of Italy by all accounts, forasmuch as the grass continues green, which it
doth not there.   This island is pleasantly laid out in hills,
and vales and rising grounds, hath plenty of excellent
springs and fine rivulets, and many delightful landscapes
of rocks and promontories, and adjacent lands.   The provisions are very good, so are the fruits, which are quite
neglected, though vines sprout up of themselves to an extraordinary size, and seem as natural to this soil as to
any I ever saw.   The town of Newport contains about
six thousand souls, and is the most thriving place in all
America for bigness.   It is very pretty, and pleasantly
situated.   I was never more agreeably surprised than at
the first sight of the town and harbor."

Soon after his arrival, the Dean purchased a
country seat and farm about three miles from
Newport, and there erected a house which he
named Whitehall.   He was admitted a freeman
of the Colony, at the General Assembly, in May,
1729.   He resided at Newport about two years
and a half, and often preached at Trinity Church.
Though he was obliged to return to Europe without effecting his original design, yet his visit was
of great utility in imparting an impulse to the lite-
rature of our country, particularly in Rhode-Island,

and Connecticut. During his residence on the Island of Rhode-Island, he meditated and composed his *Alciphron*, or Minute Philosopher, and tradition says, principally at a place about half a mile southerly from Whitehall. There, in the most elevated part of the Hanging Rocks, (so called,) he found a natural alcove, roofed and open to the south, commanding at once a beautiful view of the ocean and the circumjacent islands. This place is said to have been his favorite retreat. His Minute Philosopher was published in London, in 1732, shortly after his return. This acute and ingenious defence of the Christian religion, is written in a series of dialogues after the model of Plato. It contains many allusions to the scenery about his residence on Rhode-Island. In the introduction, he alludes, with the resignation of a Christian philosopher, to the miscarriage of his plan in founding a College. He says :

" I flattered myself, Theages, that before this time I might have been able to have sent you an agreeable account of the success of the affair that brought me into this remote corner of the country. But instead of this, I should now give the detail of the miscarriage, if I did not choose to entertain you with some incidents which have helped to make me easy under the circumstance which I could neither obviate nor foresee. Events are not always in our power, but it always is to make a good use of the very worst. And I must needs own, the course and event of this affair gave me opportunity for reflections that make me some amends for a great loss of time, pains

5

and expense. For several months past, I enjoyed much
liberty and leisure in this distant retreat."

To Bishop Berkeley, the literary institutions of
New-England are much indebted. He visited
Cambridge, Massachusetts, in 1731, and during his
residence at Newport, augmented the library of
Harvard College by valuable donations of the
Latin and Greek classics. To Yale College, he
presented eight hundred and eighty volumes, and,
on his departure from Newport, he gave the Whitehall estate, consisting of his mansion and one hundred acres of land, for three scholarships in Latin
and Greek. After his return to England, in 1733,
he sent a magnificent organ, as a donation to
Trinity Church, in Newport, which is still in constant use, and bears an inscription, which perpetuates the generosity of the donor.

Parliament having failed to afford him that assistance for the establishment of a College, which
had been promised, his project miscarried. After
he had spent more than seven years of the prime
of his life, and a large part of his private fortune
in endeavors to accomplish it, he returned to
England.

In 1734, he was raised to the See of Cloyne, and,
twelve years after, he refused the offer from lord
Chesterfield of a translation to the Bishopric of
Clogher. In the discharge of his high office, his gen-

erosity was conspicuous in the sacrifices he made, as well as in the tokens of his beneficence which he scattered around him. When, in consequence of the infirmities of age, he was unable to attend to his episcopal duties, he was unwilling to receive the emoluments of his Bishopric, and generously signed over the demense lands to be renewed at a yearly rent of two hundred pounds sterling, which sum, by his orders, was distributed among the poor. In 1752, he retired to Oxford, that he might pass the remainder of his days in learned leisure, and for the purpose of superintending the education of his son.

This excellent man died suddenly and calmly at Oxford, January 14, 1753, in the seventy-third year of his age.

Berkeley was endued with great powers of mind, and possessed of vast stores of erudition. His intellectual and moral qualities conspired to form in him a character of high and attractive excellence. The learned Bishop Atterbury said of him: " So much understanding, so much knowledge, so much innocence, and such humility, I did not think had been the portion of any but angels, until I saw this gentleman." Pope, who, as a friend, knew him well, describes him as possessed of " every virtue under Heaven."

The following verses were written by Bishop Berkeley, during his residence in Newport.

" On the prospect of planting Arts and Learning in America.

" The muse, disgusted at an age and clime,
    Barren of every glorious theme,
In distant lands now waits a better time,
    Producing subjects worthy fame :

" In happy climes, where from the genial sun
    And virgin earth fresh scenes ensue,
The force of art by nature seems outdone,
    And fancied beauties by the true :

" In happy climes, the seat of innocence,
    Where nature guides and virtue rules,
Where men shall not impose for truth and sense
    The pedantry of courts and schools :

" There shall be sung another golden age,
    The rise of empire and of arts,
The good and great inspiring epic rage,
    The wisest heads and noblest hearts.

" Not such as Europe breeds in her decay ;
    Such as she bred when fresh and young,
When heavenly flame did animate the clay
    By future ages shall be sung."

" Westward the course of empire takes its way :
    The *four* first acts already past,
A *fifth* shall close the drama with the day ;
    Time's noblest offspring is the last."

Note D—p. 20.

The following extract is from the letter sent by the First Baptist Church in Boston, to the Congregational Church in Cambridge, when Mr. Condy was to be ordained.

" *To the Church of Christ in Cambridge, under the pastoral care of the Rev. Mr. Nathaniel Appleton.*

" *Honored and beloved in the Lord:*

" This is to request you to send your Reverend Elders and Messengers to assist in the ordination of our elected Pastor, on the second Wednesday in February next. A request of the like tenor with this we have made to the churches in Boston, under the care of the Rev. Messrs. Webster and Gray, and Mr. William Hooper.

" Honored and beloved, we heartily wish you all spiritual blessings in Christ Jesus, the glorious head of the Church. We are, in behalf and by order of the Church, your affectionate brethren in the Gospel.

> " SHEM DROWNE, Deacon.
> " JOHN CALLENDER,*
> " JAMES BOUND,
> " BENJ. LANDON,
> " JOHN PROCTOR."

* This gentleman was the father of the subject of this Memoir.

The following is an extract from the manuscript journal of Rev.' John Comer, A. B., who was the predecessor of Rev. John Callender in the pastoral care of the first Baptist Church in Newport.

"January 31, 1725. This day I was baptised by the Rev. Mr. Elisha Callender, and was admitted into full communion with the Baptist Church in Boston, having before waited on the Rev. Mr. Appleton, of Cambridge, and discoursed with him on the point of baptism, together with my resolution—upon which he signified I might, notwithstanding, maintain my communion in his church: by which I discovered the candor and catholic temper of his spirit."

Mr. Comer's manuscript journal, two volumes folio, is now deposited in the cabinet of the Rhode-Island Historical Society. It is a curious production, giving an account of all the remarkable events with which he became acquainted, interspersed with prayers, religious reflections, &c. Mr. Comer had formed the design of writing the history of the American Baptists, and had collected many useful materials for this purpose, which were of great advantage to Edwards, Backus, and Benedict in their histories. For an account of this excellent man, we refer the reader to Backus, vol. 2, p. 66, 111 ; Benedict, vol. 1, p. 497.

NOTE E.—p. 22

Biographical notice of Rev. Nathaniel Clap.

The Rev. Nathaniel Clap, minister of the first Congregational Church in Newport, Rhode-Island, was born in Dorchester, Massachusetts, January, 1668. He was a descendant from one of the first planters in Massachusetts. He was graduated at Harvard College, in 1690, and while he was young his praise was in the churches, for his piety, learning, and pulpit talents. He began to preach in Newport, 1695, and in the midst of many discouragements, continued his labors till a church was formed, of which he was ordained pastor, November 3, 1720. He was minister in Newport near fifty years, and continued his pastoral care over the first Congregational Church till his death. When Mr. Whitefield arrived at Newport from Charleston, in the year 1740, he called upon Mr. Clap, and he speaks of him as the most venerable man he ever beheld. "He looked," says Mr. Whitefield, "like a good old puritan, and gave me an idea of what stamp those men were, who first settled New-England. His countenance was very heavenly, and he prayed most affectionately for a blessing on my coming to Rhode-Island. I could not but think, that I was sitting by one of the patriarchs."— *Whitefield's Journal.*

Dean Berkeley was intimate with Mr. Clap, and often spoke of his good deeds and exemplary character. He said, "Before I saw *father Clap*, I thought the Bishop of Rome had the most grave aspect of any man I ever saw, but really the minister of Newport has the most venerable appearance." Mr. Clap died October 30, 1745, in the seventy-eighth year of his age.

NOTE F—p. 23.

Mary Callender, daughter of the subject of this Memoir, was born in Newport, Dec. 12, 1731. She was about sixteen years of age when her father died; and soon after his decease, at the request of his friends, Joseph Jacob and wife, she became an inmate in their family. At the age of twenty, she became a member of the first Baptist Church, of which her father had been pastor. In the year 1762, she united with the Society of Friends, and in the 37th year of her age she became a preacher in that denomination. November 11th, 1778, she was married in Providence to Joseph Mitchell, a worthy member of the Society of Friends. In 1787, she removed to Nantucket. She quietly departed this life June 26, 1810, in the 78th year of her age. A short account of her life has been published, written by herself, with selections from some of her writings. She sustained, during the whole of her life, a most exemplary Christian character, and was held in great esteem by the Society of Friends, and by all who had the pleasure of her acquaintance.

In her account of her life, Mary Mitchell frequently speaks in the most affectionate terms of her parents. In page 9, she says:

" My father was much beloved and respected by people of all ranks that were acquainted with him; he being a person of an enlarged mind, embraced the virtues of every denomination, and lived in strict friendship with many worthy persons, from whom he differed in some religious sentiments. Among this number was Joseph Jacob and his truly virtuous wife; *these* were sensible of his worth; and my dear father's removal by death was justly esteemed by many, a public loss, he possessing qualifications for much usefulness. My dear mother was a virtuous woman, a pattern of patience, humility and resignation to the dispensations of Providence. She, with my dear father, experienced many seasons of adversity; she survived him many years, and died in sweet composure of mind, and no doubt is now at rest with the Lord."

The following account of Mary Callender is extracted from a letter which the editor has received from the learned Dr. Benjamin Waterhouse, late Professor in Harvard University, &c. &c.

" The sensible and pious *Mary Callender,* who became a public preacher in the Society of Friends, had the meek and quiet spirit of her father. Not long after her father's death, this offspring of a regularly ordained minister of the gospel, united herself with that religious Society. In Newport, there was a worthy, opulent, and very respectable member of that denomination of Christians,

named Joseph Jacob, advanced in life, who had four or
five neat and well behaved negro domestics, bound together by duty, respect and gratitude ; a pleasant picture
of patriarchal government, without fear and without reproach. But being all blacks, yet natives, it left the
master and his wife alone in the parlor and garden ; when
he invited Mary Callender to become their parlor com-
panion, and she did so to mutual satisfaction, exhibiting
a respectable picture of *father and daughter*, waited on
by black female slaves, who wore the plain, neat garb of
Quakers. The family was singular, and every thing
very decorous, relatively respectable, and marked by
humble wisdom. To see the negro women, with their
black hoods and blue aprons, walking at a respectful distance behind their master to meeting, was not an un-
pleasant sight in those days. Friend Jacob himself was
somewhat *unique* in his habits and manners. Easy in his
circumstances, and intellectual in his tastes, he filled up
his liberal leisure in watching the wind, his clock and his
weather glasses. At that day, he was the only person on
Rhode-Island who owned a thermometer. When very
cold, or very warm, he was the oracle of the atmosphere,
and of time-pieces ; for every one had recourse to him as
the prime regulator ; and when passing along to meeting
with his uniform step, people in his way consulted their
clocks and watches, without speaking to him.

" This steady follower of George Fox, though a grave
and rather silent man, had, it is presumed, no small grati-
fication in being if not *Sir Oracle*, at least *Friend Oracle*. His house was the pattern of neatness, order and
quiet, and a very proper residence for the nun-like Mary
Callender ; and in this pleasant greenhouse grew up and
prospered that fair lily of Quakerism, who sprang origin-

ally from a Baptist stock. She was not a *cactus grandi-florus*, but the modest *lily of the valley*, with qualities of the sensitive plant ; and yet she thought it her duty to proclaim, in the most public parts of the city of Newport, a mission from heaven ! I myself heard her in the open streets, call the people to repentance—exclaiming, *"Repent—repent! for the kingdom of heaven is at hand!"* She was accompanied by a grave man and woman, selected, if I mistake not, by the monthly meeting or elders. But she never raised a crowd of people around her. They rather shut their doors and windows, and considered it an *hallucination*, than a commission from heaven. They were pained, and lamented to see a tall, slender, well-looking woman, of middle age and respectable connections, suffering under a mistake. Some of the common people remarked, that had the commission come from heaven, the Lord would have given her a stronger voice and a bolder manner. I myself thought it a natural idea. Her second father by adoption, the wise and wary Joseph Jacob, had died a few years before, and left her alone, with no other guide than her own enthusiastic feelings operating on a feeble frame, and one would have supposed a timid disposition ; for there was no wildness in her manner, or any thing like rant in her utterance. I have conjectured that this was the fine feeling of her pious father, divested of his correct judgment ; who, had he lived, might have said to her, "Mary ! be not righteous overmuch, neither be thou overwise ; for why shouldst thou destroy thyself?"

" Does this character of the daughter throw any light on that of the father ? My esteemed friend, Moses Brown, that chronicle of truth, must have known her and her friend Jacob. If it were judicious to give the characters of Miton's two daughters, it cannot be too much out of the way to mention these particulars of the offspring of the Rev. John Callender.*

"Henry Collins, a wealthy merchant and a man of taste, the Lorenzo de Medicis of Rhode-Island, caused a painting to be made of parson Callender, as well as some other divines, as Hitchcock, Clap, and Dean Berkeley. I conjecture that the portrait you mention is the very one that I often admired in the Collins collection."†

* The venerable Moses Brown died September 6, 1836, aged ninety-seven years, eleven months and fourteen days. He was a liberal bene-factor of Brown University, of the Seminary belonging to the Friends, erected in Providence in 1818, and of various benevolent institutions. He was a man of vigorous intellect, of sterling integrity, of simple manners, and of unfeigned piety. In his old age he enjoyed an unusual share of health, and the powers of his mind were very little impaired. At the time of his decease he was one of the Vice Presidents of the Rhode-Island Historical Society.

† This fine original portrait, supposed to have been executed by Smi-bert, is now in the possession of Henry Bull, Esq., of Newport.

CALLENDER'S

HISTORICAL DISCOURSE.

Note.—In order to preserve entire the original form of Mr. Callender's Historical Discourse, the notes of the edition are all of them placed in the Appendix, except two or three which are intended to correct errors, into which the author had fallen with regard to dates, &c. The title page and dedication of the former edition are also retained.

AN

HISTORICAL DISCOURSE,

ON THE

CIVIL AND RELIGIOUS AFFAIRS

OF THE COLONY OF

RHODE-ISLAND AND PROVIDENCE PLANTATIONS,

IN NEW-ENGLAND, IN AMERICA,

FROM THE FIRST SETTLEMENT, 1638, TO THE

END OF THE FIRST CENTURY.

BY JOHN CALLENDER, A. M.

JOSHUA, xxii. 22.—The LORD God of Gods, the LORD God of Gods, he knoweth, and Israel shall know, if it be in rebellion, or in transgression against the Lord.
PSALMS, cxlv. 4.—One generation shall praise thy name to another, and shall declare thy mighty acts.

DEDICATION.

WILLIAM CODDINGTON, ESQ.

Sir—It is not barely to give you a public testimony of my gratitude for many personal favors, nor yet of that esteem and respect which all men bear you, for your singular equity and benevolence, not only in private life, but in all the various offices, in which you have served and adorned your country ; that I prefix your name to these papers : but because an attempt to recover some account of this happy Island, and to make a religious improvement of the merciful providences of God towards it, is justly due to the lineal representative of that worthy gentleman, who was the great instrument of its original settlement.

Your honored grandfather, William Coddington, Esq., was chosen in *England* to be an *Assistant* of the Colony of the *Massachusetts Bay*, A. D. 1629, and in 1630 came over to *New-England* with the

7

Governor and the Charter, &c., after which he was several times rechosen to that honorable and important office. He was for some time treasurer of the Colony. He was with the chiefest in all public charges, " and a principal merchant in Boston," where he built the first brick house.

In the year 1637, when the contentions ran so high in the country, he was grieved at the proceedings of the Court against Mr. Wheelwright and others. And when he found that his opposition to those measures was ineffectual, he entered his protest, " that his dissent might appear to succeeding times;" and though he was in the fairest way to be great, in the *Massachusetts*, as to outward things, yet he voluntarily quitted his advantageous situation at *Boston*, his large property and his improvements at *Braintree*, for peace sake, and that he might befriend, protect, and assist the pious people, who were meditating a removal from that Colony, on account of their religious differences.

Here, when the people first incorporated themselves a body politic on this Island, they chose him to be their judge or chief ruler, and continued to elect him annually to be their Governor for seven

years together, till the Patent took place, and the
Island was incorporated with *Providence Plantations.*

In the year 1647, he assisted in forming the body
of laws, which has been the basis of our constitution and government ever since; and the next
year being chosen Governor of the Colony, de-
clined the office.

In 1651, he had a commission from the supreme
authority then in *England,* to be Governor of the
Island, pursuant to a power reserved in the *Patent:*
but the people being jealous " the commission might
affect their lands and liberties as secured to them
by the Patent," he readily laid it down on the first
notice from *England* that he might do so; and for
their further satisfaction and contentment, he, by
a writing under his hand, obliged himself to make
a formal surrender of all right and title to any of
the lands, more than his proportion in common
with the other inhabitants, whenever it should be
demanded.

After that, he seems to have retired much from
public business, till toward the latter end of his
days, when he was again divers times prevailed

with to take the government upon him ; as he did particularly 1678, when he died November 1, in the seventy-eighth year of his age, *a good man, full of days.* Thus, after he had the honor to be the first judge and Governor of this Island, " after he had spent much of his estate and the prime of his life in propagating plantations," he died Governor of the Colony—in promoting the welfare and the prosperity of the little commonwealth, which he had in a manner founded.

If there was any opposition at any time to any of his measures, or if he met with any ungrateful returns from any he had served, it was no more than what several of the other first excellent Governors of the other *New English* colonies met with, from a people made froward by the circumstances of a wilderness, and over-jealous of their privileges. A free people will always be jealous of their privileges, and history abounds with examples of the mistakes and ingratitude occasioned by that jealousy.

If the following Discourse has done any justice to the memory and character of the pious people who first settled this Colony, or if it has any tendency to promote the true original ends of this

Plantation, I am sure of your patronage. And as to what relates to some articles, different from your judgment and practice in religious matters, the generosity and candor you inherit from your great ancestors, will easily bear with me, endeavoring to vindicate my own opinions on such an occasion.

I hope there are few or no errors in the matters of fact related, or the dates that are assigned; to prevent any mistakes, I have carefully reviewed the public records, and my other materials; this review has brought to my knowledge or remembrance, many things that were not mentioned in the pulpit, which however it seemed ought not to be omitted.

I designed to have put all the additions and enlargements, in the form of notes, for my own ease, but have been persuaded to weave as many of them as were proper into the body of the Discourse, as what is generally most pleasing to the reader. I am very sensible, several things will be thought too minute or personal by strangers, but the descendants of the persons concerned, and the inhabitants of the Colony, will readily pardon me.

And some other things which are familiarly known among ourselves, will be necessary to others.

It is much to be lamented that many valuable manuscripts of some of the first settlers here, are so soon embezzled and lost. And it is much to be wished, that some gentlemen of ingenuity and leisure, would take pains to collect as many of these old papers as can be found dispersed about. I am apt to think, that these, with the public records, would furnish materials for a *just history* of the Colony.

What is here presented to your view, will by no means supersede such a design; I rather hope it will stimulate gentlemen in every part of the Colony, to make a search after such papers, and more especially *now*, while the *New-England Chronology* is in hand, composing by a gentleman, above all exceptions universally acknowledged the best versed in the history of the country, and the most capable to give the world a just and clear idea of all our civil and religious affairs, and *who is* already so well furnished with materials from every other part of the country.

That the Most High would be pleased to bless
you with all the blessings of grace and providence,
together with your pious lady and numerous offspring, is the prayer of

    Your Honor's most obliged

        humble servant,

          JOHN CALLENDER.

Newport, on Rhode-Island, Oct. 27, 1738.

AN HISTORICAL DISCOURSE, &c.

PSALMS, LXXVII. 10, 11, 12.

I will remember the years of the right hand of the Most High. I will remember the work of the Lord, surely I will remember thy wonders of old, I will meditate also of all thy work, and talk of thy doings.

As it is now more than a century, since the lands within the present patent, or charter of this Colony, began to be settled by Englishmen, and inhabited by Christians, our ancestors; and as this day is just an hundred years since the Indian Sachems, *Miantonomy** and the ancient *Canonicus*, his uncle and guardian, signed the grant of this Island, to Mr. Coddington and his friends united with him; and as Mr. John Clark, the founder under God, and the first elder of this Church, and its liberal benefactor, was a principal instrument in negotiating the purchase and settlement of the

---

*The name of this Sachem is usually spelt in the printed books, Miantonimoh, but in all the manuscripts, Myantonomy, or Miantonome, or Miantonomu, and the name is so pronounced by the people who take the sound by tradition, and not from the books, with the accent on the last syllable but one.

9

Island, as he was likewise afterward, in obtaining and maintaining the old patent, and procuring the present charter; I thought it would be but proper to defer our Lecture, which in course fell out on yesterday, to this time; and now I propose to lay before you, such an account as I have been able to collect, of the occasion and the manner of our first settlement, together with a short view of the civil and religious history, and the present state of the Colony. And then to entertain you with such reflections as the subject will suggest, and such remarks as may serve to dispose and assist us, to a religious improvement of those memorable occurrences.

I confess the account I have been able to collect is very lame and imperfect, and for that reason I should have laid aside the design, if I had not thought it in reality a duty, to recollect and review so much as we can of the merciful providence of God, in the settling and preserving this Colony; and that we ought to remember the years of the right hand of the Most High, the works of the Lord, and the wonders of old, to meditate of his work, and talk of his doings.

And here, in order to lay before you some account of the occasion and manner of our first settlement, and the conduct of Divine Providence towards us ever since, it may be proper, previously to mention a few things relating to the settlement of New-England in general.

And that we may take things from the beginning, be pleased to observe that October 12, 1492,* this part of the world since called America, before that wholly unknown to the rest, was first discovered by Christopher Columbus, a Genoese, in the service of the king of Spain. The Pope soon after, generously bestowed the new world on the Spaniards; they made many successful voyages, and many great conquests and settlements in the southern parts of the new found world. Their success and the immense riches they carried home to Europe, did, in process of time, excite other nations to put in for a share with them. Among the rest the English (who had narrowly missed the advantages of the first discovery) besides their enterprises on the Spaniards, made many successive attempts to discover and settle in North America.

In 1578 or 1579, there was a patent granted by Queen Elizabeth for six years to Sir H. Gilbert, to

---

* Where several writers give the same account, 'tis needless to quote any one in particular, as 'tis also, where the account is taken from a comparison of many authors, with one another. However, I have followed the dates in the New-England Chronology, where the most material facts are collected, and placed in the truest light, and the dates fixed with the greatest accuracy and exactness. The reader will observe many expressions marked " " ; these are the very words of the authorities I follow, and which I choose to make use of as often as conveniently might be.

plant and inhabit some northern parts of America, unpossessed by any Prince with whom she had any alliance.

March 25, 1584, Queen Elizabeth granted to Sir W. Raleigh a patent for foreign parts not possessed by any Christian Prince. And the same year, he took possession of the country to the westward of Roanoke, and called it Virginia, in honor of his mistress. He sent three several colonies to settle in those parts, who all failed. As did Capt. Gosnold, in a like attempt to settle in what is since called New-England, which he first discovered in 1602. And several other attempts met with the like ill success.

April 10, 1606, King James divided Virginia into two colonies, which were called South and North, the first between 34 and 41 degrees north, and the last between 38 and 45, and they were not to settle within an hundred miles of one another. By 1611, the Southern or London company, had made an effectual settlement; while the Northern or Plymouth company were almost discouraged at their repeated disappointments. However, Judge Popham, Sir Ferdinando Gorges, and others, continued their attempts and their designs, till Divine Providence began a settlement within their jurisdiction, without their knowledge or contrivance.

It is acknowledged, on all hands, the first settlements of New-England were a consequence of the disputes which attended the Reformation in England ; and therefore we must observe, that during this time, viz. 1517, learning having revived all over Europe, the Reformation was begun by Luther, and others in Germany, and carried on in several parts of Christendom, particularly in England, where, after a long struggle, it was was finally established, by act of Parliament, under Queen Elizabeth, who began to reign November 17, 1558.

As the whole Christian religion had been corrupted and disfigured by the inventions and impositions of Popery, in a long course of time, it is so far from being to be wondered at, that it could not but be expected that many, who were justly and equally offended, at the horrid corruptions of Popery, should yet be unable entirely to agree in their sentiments, of what things were to be reformed, or how far they should carry the Reformation at the first. And yet this was every where a great and unhappy *remora* to that glorious work, and gave their enemies a very considerable advantage, which they well knew how, and failed not to improve to the utmost.

The effects of these divisions, and the animosities with which they were maintained, were felt in England, not only in the beginning of the Reformation, but after it was established, and even ever since to this day. Among the Reformers in Queen

Elizabeth's reign (many of whom had been exiles in Queen Mary's persecution, and so had more opportunities to see and converse with the foreign Protestants) there were many who sought to carry the Reformation, farther in some points than had been done in King Edward's time. They sought to take away every thing they imagined had the color of superstition, and to make the Bible their real rule in worship and discipline, as well as in faith. These were presently called Puritans, as pretending to seek a purer church state and a farther reformation than the other party thought was necessary or expedient.

Those had not the same exceptions to many things the Puritans scrupled; and beside, thought it was but good policy to make as few and as little changes and alterations as possible, especially in the ceremonies, which most powerfully affect the vulgar, in order to draw in the bulk of the clergy and the nation to favor the other alterations, which all of them esteemed to be of the most importance. And the Queen zealously espousing this party, turned the balance in their favor; and accordingly for some years the whole nation, in effect, came to church, though the times were far from being settled.

The Puritans, it seems, had few or no objections to the articles of faith, but they chiefly objected against the liturgy, the ceremonies, and the constitution and discipline. But, however, they were not perfectly agreed among themselves; while the much larger part of them, fathers of those since called Presbyterians, generally strove to keep their places in the church, without conforming to some of the most offensive ceremonies, and by voluntary agreement among themselves, sought to remedy, and supply what they thought was amiss or wanting, in the parliamentary establishment; others of them, fathers of those since called Independents and Congregationalists, separated wholly from the public worship, in the parish churches, and sought a thorough alteration in the whole form and constitution of the church, and to lay aside the liturgy and all the ceremonies together.

Queen Elizabeth kept a watchful and jealous eye over them all, as fearing, and being determined against all farther alterations in religious matters. And subscription and conformity, being at times pressed harder, as the friends to the Puritans were out of power, some of them, especially of those called Separatists, had been driven out of England, and at length there was a church of the independent scheme, formed at Amsterdam, in Holland. In the reign of King James, (whom the Puritans expected to be a patron to them, as he had been educated in Scotland, and had openly censured the Church of England,) those things which offended them, were carried with an higher hand. In the years 1608, and 1609, several more of them in the north

of England, removed to Holland, and a number of
them settled at Leyden under the pastoral care of
Mr. John Robinson, (afterwards the father of
Plymouth colony,) in hopes to enjoy that liberty
of their consciences, in a strange land, they were
denied at home.

Here they continued eleven or twelve years, till,
for many reasons, they began to meditate a removal, and chose to seek an asylum somewhere in
North America, near Hudson's river. They had a
long and tedious treaty with the southern or Virginia Company, who might reasonably expect
greater sobriety, patience and industry, from a
people of such a character, and in such circumstances, and who had such views and designs of
their own, than they had found in such other people
as they could prevail on to transport themselves
into a wilderness. However, the factions and dis-
turbances in the Company, and other causes, delayed the affairs for some time, till 1619, in the
fall, they obtained a Patent for the land, but they
could not obtain a legal assurance of the liberty of
their consciences. However, they determined at
length to remove, depending on some general
promises of connivance, if they behaved themselves
peaceably, and hoping that the distance and re-
moteness of the place, as well as the public service
they should do the King and Kingdom, would prevent their being disturbed.

After encountering many difficulties and discouragements, from the nature and circumstances
of their voyage, and from the treachery of some of
the undertakers, they arrived at Cape Cod, on the
9th of November, 1620. Here they found their
Patent useless, this place being within the bounds
of the New-England or Plymouth Company; and
yet necessity obliged them to set down thereabout.
They did, therefore, two days after, incorporate
themselves a body politic, and having made such a
search of the adjacent country as their circumstances would allow, at that time of the year, they
began their settlement, about Christmas, at a place
called by the Indians, Patuxet; by them named
New Plymouth. Infinite, almost, were the hardships and distresses of the ensuing winter, in which
near half the Company died for want of necessaries.
However, through the merciful providence of God,
they maintained their ground, and through many
difficulties, which they overcame by patience and
the divine blessing, they increased to three hundred
souls in nine years after, when they obtained a
Patent from the New-England Company, the 13th
of January, 1629—30.

In that period, there had been many successless
attempts to make settlements in New-England, for
the sake of trade and husbandry only, as if Divine
Providence had reserved the place for those who
soon after took possession of it. The success of

the Plymouth planters began to excite the Puritans, all over England, to meditate a removal to
those parts of the world, in order to enjoy the liberty
of worshipping God according to their consciences.
There was no ground at all left them to hope for
any condescension or indulgence to their scruples,
but uniformity was pressed with harder measures
than ever. A great part of the nation was alarmed
with the apprehensions of Arminianism, and that
even Popery itself was approaching; yea, the civil
affairs, and the peace of the nation, began to be
embroiled and interrupted by the false politics and
bad counsels of the unhappy Prince on the throne;
so that New-England began to be looked on by
them as a place of refuge; and it is said, that some
who proved principal actors in the changes and
events that followed, had even determined to
transport themselves here, had they not been unaccountably restrained by authority. This is certain, the same principles in some persons, which
had rendered their stay uneasy at home, and which
at first refused them a legal toleration in the wilds
of America, made their leaving the Kingdom as
difficult as possible. Whereas, could good policy
have prevailed over bigotry, it would have appeared a good expedient for them, thus to clear the
Kingdom of the disaffected and nonconformists,
and with them make such an effectual plantation,
as promised a great addition to the trade and riches,
and power of the Kingdom, and greatly enlarged
its territory.

Mr. White, of Dorchester, the father of the Massachusetts Colony, encouraged Mr. R. Conant, who had, on disgust, removed from Plymouth to Nantasket, to continue in the country, with the promise of men, and all things necessary for another plantation. Whereupon, this gentleman, 1625, removed to Cape Ann, and the next year to Naumkeak, since called Salem. March 19, 1627—8, the Council for New-England signed the Massachusetts Patent, and March 4, 1628—9, the King confirms it by Ca harter which included liberty of conscience. The nonconformists, so called, are busily employed about their intended expedition. In 1628, they send Mr. Endicot, with some people, to begin and prepare the way for them, and the next year they send Mr. Higginson and many more; and, 1630, Governor Winthorp, Deputy Governor Dudley, with the Assistants, the Charter, and fifteen hundred people, and all necessaries, came over and made effectual settlements at Charlestown, Watertown, Dorchester, Boston, &c.; and more of their friends coming over to them, in the following years, the new settlements increased and prospered, notwithstanding the many difficulties and hardships which must necessarily attend the planting such a remote wilderness.

As the country was more fully discovered, the lands on Connecticut river grew so famous for their fruitfulness, and convenience to keep cattle, that great numbers from New-Town, Dorchester, &c.,

removed there, under the conduct of Mr. Hains,
Mr. Hopkins, Mr. Ludlow, and Mr. Hooker, &c.,
and through inexpressible hardships, through
famine, and weariness, and perils of the enemy,
they at length settled at Hartford, 1635 and 1636,
which was the beginning of Connecticut colony;
and, in 1637, New-Haven colony was begun by a
people directly from England, under the leading
of Mr. Eaton, and Mr. Davenport, &c. Thus the
four grand colonies of New-England were begun in
a few years, and some faint attempts likewise made
to settle in the eastward parts, in the province of
Maine, &c., for the sake of trade and fishery, and
by some of the people who afterwards came here.
Which brings me to the more immediate occasion
of the settlement of this Colony, and the manner
in which it was brought about and accomplished.
It is allowed, by all sides, the religious differences
among the first settlers of the Massachusetts
Colony, gave rise to this colony, and the settling of
this Island.

Almost all the first settlers of New-England
were Puritans. The people at Plymouth were
generally of that sort called Separatists, and those
of Boston generally had lived in the communion of
the Church of England, though they scrupled conforming to some of the ceremonies. But these
being come to so great a distance from the Bishops'
power, could well enough agree in the same forms
of worship, and method of discipline with the church

at Plymouth, and a mixed form of church government was generally set up. Though they had seemed well enough united, by the common zeal against the ceremonies, yet now they were removed from the ecclesiastical courts, with a patent which gave them liberty of conscience, a variety of opinions as to several points, before not so much regarded, and perhaps not thought of, now began to be visible, and operate with considerable effects. It is no wonder such differences in opinion arose among them, as had been the case before among the Protestants in general. It was the avowed opinion of some among them of chiefest note and authority, (Mr. Hooker,) "that there were two great reserves for inquiry in that age of the world: first, wherein the spiritual rule of our Lord's kingdom doth consist, and after what manner it is revealed, managed and maintained in the souls of his people; the second, after what order the government of our Lord's kingdom is to be externally managed and maintained in his church."—*Magnalia B. 3. p.* 66.

Notwithstanding which, the chief leaders, and the major part of the people, soon discovered themselves as fond of uniformity, and as loath to allow liberty of conscience to such as differed from themselves, as those from whose power they had fled. Notwithstanding all their sufferings and complaints in England, they seemed incapable of mutual forbearance; perhaps they were afraid of provoking

the higher powers at home, if they countenanced
other sects; and perhaps those who differed from
them took the more freedom, in venting and pres-
sing their peculiar opinions, from the safety and
protection they expected, under a charter that had
granted liberty of conscience.

In reality, the true grounds of liberty of conscience were not then known, or embraced by any
sect or party of Christians; all parties seemed to
think that as they only were in the possession of
the truth, so they alone had a right to restrain, and
crush all other opinions, which they respectively
called error and heresy, where they were the most
numerous and powerful; and in other places they
pleaded a title to liberty and freedom of their consciences. And yet, at the same time, all would disclaim persecution for conscience sake, which has
something in it so unjust and absurd, so cruel and
impious, that all men are ashamed of the least im-
putation of it. A pretence of the public peace, the
preservation of the Church of Christ from infection,
and the obstinacy of the heretics, are always made
use of, to excuse and justify that, which, stripped of
all disguises, and called by its true name, the light
of nature, and the laws of Christ Jesus condemn
and forbid, in the most plain and solemn manner.
Mr. R. Williams and Mr. J. Clark, two fathers of
this Colony, appear among the first who publicly
avowed that Jesus Christ is king in his own kingdom, and that no others had authority over his

subjects, in the affairs of conscience and eternal salvation. So that it was not singular or peculiar in those people at the Massachusetts, to think themselves bound in conscience to use the sword of the civil magistrate to open the understandings of heretics, or cut them off from the State, that they might not infect the church or injure the public peace. These were not the only people who thought they were doing God good service, when smiting their brethren and fellow-servants. All other Christian sects acted generally, as if they thought this was the very best service they could do to God, and the most effectual way to promote the gospel of peace, and prove themselves the true and genuine disciples of Jesus Christ—of Jesus Christ, who hath declared, his kingdom was not of this world, who had commanded his disciples to call no man master on earth, who had forbidden them to exercise lordship over each other's consciences, who had required them to let the tares grow with the wheat till the harvest, and who had, in fine, given mutual love, peace, long-suffering, and kindness, as the badge and mark of his religion.

Mr. Roger Williams, a minister, who came over to Salem, 1630, had, on a disgust, removed to Plymouth, where he was an assistant to their minister, Mr. Smith, for two years. And being disgusted likewise at Plymouth, returned back to Salem, where he was chosen by the people to succeed Mr. Skelton, in 1634. The magistrates opposed his settlement there, as they had done before. They made great objections to his principles, and it is said some wordly things helped to increase the animosities that soon prevailed against him; though Mr. Williams appears, by the whole course and tenor of his life and conduct here, to have been one of the most disinterested men that ever lived, a most pious and heavenly minded soul. He was charged with holding it "unlawful for an unregenerate man to pray, or a regenerate man to pray with him;" "that it was unlawful for the magistrate to meddle with the breaches of the first table;" and that he insisted on an unlimited toleration, or liberty of conscience; from whence they inferred him an advocate for licentiousness, which the good man's soul abhorred, "and ever disclaimed." However, on these accounts, and for teaching the Patent was sinful, (in what sense and how truly is very obvious,) for opposing the oath of fidelity, (not out of disloyalty to the King, but on account of the nature of an oath, which he thought, as a sacred thing, ought not to be forced on all men promiscuously, whether in a state of grace or nature,) "and for separating from, and renouncing communion with all the churches in the land, and even with his own, for not joining with him therein;"—for these things, he was at length banished the Colony, as a disturber of the peace of the church and commonwealth; and, as he says, "a bull of excommunication was sent after him in his absence."

He came away to *Secunke*, since called Reho-
both, where he procured a grant of lands, from
Ousamequin, or Massasoiet, the chief Sachem of
Pokanokik. But being desired to remove from
thence, which was within the jurisdiction of New-
Plymouth, "he had several treaties with Myantonomy and Canonicus, the *Nantygansick*, or Narraganset Sachems, in the years 1634 and 1635, who
assured him he should not want for land for a settlement;" Divine Providence giving him wonderfully great favor in the eyes of the Sachems. And
in the spring of the year 1634–5,* he came over the
river to a place called by the Indians Mooshausick,
and by him named Providence, " in a sense of God's
merciful providence to him in his distress." And
several of his friends following him, they planted
there. The authority and power of Miantonomy
awed all the Indians round, to assist and succor
these few feeble and helpless Englishmen, thus cast
out by their brethren, in a strange land. However,
we must (to be impartial) own that their being
Englishmen, was a real security and protection to

---

* Here is an error of one year. It was in the spring of
1635–6, or what would now be called 1636, that Roger
Williams came over Seekonk River, and settled at Mooshausick or Providence. The precise day or month cannot be ascertained. The earliest record of his being here
is under date of July 26, 1636, O. S. See Knowles'
Memoir of Roger Williams, p. 101—105. Savage's Winthrop, vol. 1, p. 193.—*Editor.*

them, unless the Indians had designed a general war. The English at Massachusetts employed Mr. Williams to make a league offensive and defensive with the Narraganset Indians, in the Pequot war, which followed in 1637. And the Indian Sachems, in one of their confirmations of the grants of lands to him,* express their gratitude, " for the many kindnesses and services he had continually done for them, both with their friends at Massachusetts, as also at Qunniticut, and Apaum or Plymouth." Mr. Williams also maintained a' loving correspondence with many of his old friends to the last, and was esteemed and valued by many of them; though he ever opposed, and that in print, once and again, what he called the *bloody tenent,* i. e. every kind and degree of persecution for conscience sake. The hardships and distresses of these poor exiles, are hardly to be conceived by the present generation, who, through the divine goodness, have never seen any thing like what they cheerfully endured. But Divine Providence, in which they trusted, supported them, and provided for them in their greatest straits, and wonderfully blessed their honest industry, so that in a few years they had plenty of all things necessary to their subsistence and comfort.

---

* The said writing is dated Nanhygansick, the 24th of the first month, commonly called March, the second year of our Plantation, or planting at Mooshasick or Providence.

The banishment of Mr. Williams, and the voluntary exile of many of his adherents, did not put an end to the unhappy divisions and contentions in the Massachusetts. Mr. Hains, the Governor, in 1635, did with great difficulty still and quiet the storm for the present, in the beginning of his administration; but Mr., afterwards Sir Henry Vane, jun., arriving at Boston that summer, and zealously falling in with the opinions of one party, he was by them persuaded to tarry there, (though designed for Connecticut river,) and was the next year, 1636, chosen Governor; and then the animosities and contentions were carried to a very great height; one side reproaching the other, as *Legalists* and under a covenant of works, &c., and the others calling them *Familists, Antinomians, &c.* The next year, Mr. Winthrop being rechosen Governor, with a great struggle, he strenuously exerted himself to crush and exterminate the opinions he disapproved. A synod was called for that end at New-Town, (since named Cambridge,) on the 30th of August, where eighty erroneous opinions were presented, debated, and condemned; and a court held on the 2d of October following, at the same place, banished a few of the chief persons, among those who were aspersed with those errors; and censured several that had been the most active, not, it seems, for their holding those opinions, but for their pretended seditious carriage and behavior; and the church at Boston likewise excom-

municated at least one of her members, not for
those opinions, but for denying they ever held
them, and the behavior which these heats occasioned ; and some of these, with their friends and
followers, came to this Island.

Notwithstanding such a formidable number of
errors, produced at the synod, that which these
people differed in from the others, was chiefly this,
as Mr. John Clark has briefly represented it, viz:
" Touching the covenants and in point of evidencing a man's good estate. Some (says he) pressed
hard for the covenant of works, and for sanctification to be the first and chief evidence; others
(he means himself and those who came here)
pressed as hard for the covenant of grace, that was
established on better promises, and for the evidence
of the spirit, as that which is a more sure, constant, and satisfactory witness." (*Clark's Narrative Introd.*) This account is agreeable to what
there is in those books wrote on the other side, I
have had the opportunity to consult; only they
must be allowed to express, in their own way, their
own sentiments of the opinions of the other side,
and they add such shades as darken and disfigure
the opinions of the opposite party, and set off their
own to the best advantage.

Dr. Mather thus describes the five questions debated between the synod and Mr. Cotton, (which

were the same points about which all the divisions first began;) they were " about the order of things in our union to our Lord Jesus Christ, about the influence of our faith in the application of his righteousness, about the use of our sanctification in evidencing our justification, and about the consideration of our Lord Jesus Christ, by men, yet under a covenant of works; briefly, they were the points whereon depend the grounds of our assurance for blessedness in another and better world. *Mag.* B. 7, p. 17

Mr. Neal says, " The Commonwealth was almost torn in pieces by intestine divisions, occasioned by the spreading Familistical and Antinomian errors among the people." And from the writers before him, he gives the original of the controversy, to this purpose: " The members of the church at Boston used to meet once a week, to repeat the sermons they heard on the Lord's Day, and to debate on the doctrines contained in them; those meetings being peculiar to the men, some of the zealous women thought it might be useful to them. One Mrs. Hutchinson, a gentlewoman of a bold and masculine spirit, and a great admirer of Mr. Cotton, set up one at her house. The novelty of the thing, and the fame of the woman, quickly gained her a numerous audience, and from these meetings arose all the errors that soon after overspread the country." He says she taught that believers in Christ are personally united to the spirit of God; that commands to work out our salvation with fear and trembling, belong to none but such as are under the covenant of works; that sanctification is not a good evidence of a good estate. She likewise set up immediate revelation about future events, to be believed as equally infallible with the scriptures; and a great many other chimeras and fancies, which, (says he,) under a pretence of exalting the free grace of God, destroyed the practical part of religion, " and opened a door to all sorts of licentiousness·" *Neal's Hist.* C. 5, p. 166.

I shall not enter into the merits of the cause; there is neither time nor occasion for it, only, I must observe, how each side ascribed to the others, consequences they imagined followed from their opinions, which they did not see or own. And particularly the people who came here, have things laid to their charge, which they utterly denied and detested equally with their antagonists. So harshly did their adversaries judge of them, as even to involve in their opinions, or the consequences of them, a denial of the resurrection of the dead, and the life everlasting; which totally subverts and' destroys Christianity, and all religion at once, which necessarily implies a future state; when yet the whole debate supposed the truth of Christianity, and the certainty of a future state; and the main question was about the method in which they might best obtain an assurance of their interest in, and their title to, the inheritance of the saints in light. The very first of the eighty errors to be tried in the synod, doth (as I remember) charge the denial of the immortality of the soul, as a consequence of the opinion, that the faculties of the soul are passive or quiescent in the work of conversion and regeneration ; when yet the synod themselves unanimously believed particular election and irresistible grace.

"The question was, by what evidence must a man proceed in taking to himself the comforts of his justification. The bigger part of the country laid the first and main stress of our comfortable evidence, on our sanctification ; but the opinionists (says Dr. Mather) were for another sort of evidence, as their chief, namely the spirit of God, by a powerful application of a promise, begetting in us, and revealing to us, a powerful assurance of our being justified." *Mag.* B. 7. p. 14.

Now, as the Doctor adds, (even on this way of stating the question, or expressing the sentiments of those called opinionists, which they would be far from acquiescing in, as expressing their full and true opinion,) " the truth might easily have united both the seopinions." But as he goes on, "they carried the matter on to a very perilous door, opened to many errors and evils, yea, to threaten a subversion of the

peaceable order in government." But they deny
and disclaim the consequences fixed on them, and
justify their own opinion and conduct, and charge
the other party with as fatal and mischievous consequences, and a conduct arbitrary and oppressive.

Besides the differences about those points, for
which these people were charged with Antinomian-
ism, what was called Familism was, perhaps, not a
little offensive. Nay, their differences in opinion
were worked up to almost a state quarrel at the
last, as Arminianism had been in Holland, and
Episcopacy was in England afterwards, and as the
Reformation still is all over Europe. The public
affairs of town and Colony were affected by these
contentions, and the Governor and Assistants put in
and out, as the one or the other side prevailed.
The whole people unhappily run into factions and
parties, in such a manner, as if contention and every
evil work had not been evidences incontestible,
that the wisdom from which they proceeded could
not be from above. But so it is, where men differ
about religion, their contentions are usually the
most sharp, and carried on with the most irreligious
heat and animosity : even though they differ about
the smallest matters, or when, as was the case
here, they differ from each other but in a very little.

A great part of the body of the people, and I am
apt to think, at the first, the majority of the town

of Boston, were of the same side the question with those people who afterwards came here. It is certain, the synod and the court were both held at New-Town, because of the disaffection of the people of Boston. The deputies of the town, at least some of them, openly espoused that party. The town, at least many of them, petitioned in their favor. And Mr. Cotton, the chief oracle then of both town and country, was confidently believed by them to be of the opinion they contended for. To which I might add the number of the people in that town, that were censured at the court.

Those who came away, were most of them long esteemed as brethren of the church, and never censured by the church at all; nay, that church did long retain some particularities, as to the brethren's power in church affairs, and their liberty to exercise their gifts in private or family meetings, and as to the subjects of infant baptism. It is certain, Mr. Wheelwright, minister to a branch of that church, at a place since called Braintree, (where the town had some lands,) was eager and zealous against the covenant of works; and was banished by the court for what was then called sedition, by the same rule which will make every dissent from, or opposition to, a majority in any religious affairs, to be sedition, and an iniquity to be punished by the judge. The minor part must always be seditious, if it be sedition to defend their

11

own religious opinions, and endeavor to confute the contrary. This maxim, once allowed, must chain men down under errors and falsehoods wherever they prevail, and even rivet their chains. On this foot, what will become of the glorious martyrs for the gospel in the first ages of it, and the holy apostles, who turned the world upside down, who turned men from darkness to light, from the gods of the nations, whom they called vanities, to the living and true God? Nay, what shall we say of our blessed Saviour himself, who says he came to send division on earth? How shall we excuse the Protestants, nay, how shall we justify the Puritans themselves, if it be seditious to oppose any religious opinions we think are false or erroneous, when the major part of the society happen to think otherwise? I must farther add, that however Mr. Cotton, at the synod, after long labor with him, disowned many of the opinions charged on these people, yet he would not condemn all the said errors in the gross, as the rest did, and there is some reason to believe that he differed from the other ministers to the last, at least in the manner of explaining these most abstruse and difficult points; if he did not continue to hold, that "union to Christ was before faith in him, and that the habit of faith proceeded or followed from our justification," which it is said, he once seemed to hold in the synod; and which was in reality the root or fountain of all the opinions so much faulted in this people. And however Mr. Cotton has in print disowned them, and they are by others charged with falsehood and calumny, in shrouding themselves under the authority of his great name ; yet they who should be owned to know their own opinions, and understand their own expressions and designs best, always persisted in it, that " Mr. Cotton was with them," or that they meant no more than they understood him to mean.

But to return. The affair was agitated in court for three days; and, some changing sides in the court, the majority was on the side of the synod, and took measures effectually to support their own opinions. Whereupon, many of the other side determined to remove, for peace sake, and to enjoy the freedom of their consciences. And Mr. John Clark, " who made the proposal, was requested, with some others, to seek out a place, and, thereupon, by reason of the suffocating heat of the summer before, he went north, to be somewhat cooler, but the winter following proving as cold, they were forced in the spring to make towards the south. So, having sought the Lord for direction, they agreed, that while their vessel was passing about a large and dangerous Cape, (Cape Cod,) they would cross over by land, having Long-Island and Delaware Bay in their eye, for the place of their residence. At Providence, Mr. R. Williams lovingly entertained them, and being consulted about

their design, readily presented two places before
them in the Narraganset Bay, the one on the main
called *Sow-wames*, (the neck since called Phebe's
Neck, in Barrington,*) and *Aquetneck*, now Rhode-
Island." And inasmuch as they were determined
to go out of every other jurisdiction, Mr. Williams
and Mr. Clark, attended with two other persons,
went to Plymouth to inquire how the case stood;
they were lovingly received, and answered, that
Sowames was the garden of their Patent. But
they were advised to settle at *Aquetneck,* and
promised to be looked on as free, and to be treated
and assisted as loving neighbors. (*Mr. J. Clark's
Nar.*) On their return, the 7th of March, 1637–8,
the people, to the number of eighteen,† incorporated themselves a body politic, and chose Mr.
Coddington their leader, to be the judge or chief

---

* Perhaps *Sowames* is properly the name of the river,
where the two Swansey rivers meet and run together for
near a mile, when they empty themselves in the Narraganset Bay, or of a small Island, where those two rivers
meet, at the bottom of New Meadow Neck, so called.

† Their names are as follow, William Coddington, John
Clark, William Hutchinson, John Coggeshall, William
Aspinwall, Samuel Wilbore, John Porter, John Sanford,
Edward Hutchinson, jun., Thomas Savage, William
Dyre, William Freeborne, Philip Shearman, John Walker,
Richard Carder, William Baulston, Edward Hutchinson,
sen., Henry Bull.

magistrate. After the same manner, Plymouth and Connecticut Colonies were forced to enter into a voluntary agreement or covenant at the first, as having no legal authority amongst them; the people here, however, immediately sought a Patent, and in a few years obtained one.

Mr. R. Williams was very instrumental in procuring the Island of the Indian sachems, and has left this account in *perpetuam rei memoriam.* " It was not price or money that could have purchased Rhode-Island, but it was obtained by love, that love and favor which that honored gentleman, Sir Henry Vane, and myself, had with the great sachem Myantonomy, about the league which I procured, between the Massachusetts English and the Narragansets in the Pequot War. This I mention, that as the truly noble Sir Henry Vane hath been so great an instrument, in the hand of God, for procuring this Island of the barbarians, as also for the procuring and confirming the Charter, it may be with all thankful acknowledgments recorded, and remembered by us, and ours who reap the sweet fruits of so great benefits, and such unheard of liberties among us." (*MS. of R. W.*) And in another manuscript, he tells us the Indians were very shy and jealous of selling the lands to any, and chose rather to make a grant of them to such as they affected, but, at the same time, expected such gratuities and rewards as made an Indian *gift* often times a very dear bargain. And the Colony, seventy years ago, 1666, averred, that though the favor Mr. Williams had with Myantonomy was the great means of procuring the grants of the land, yet the purchase had been dearer than of any lands in New-England; the reason of which might be, partly, the English inhabited between two powerful nations, the *Wampanoags* to the north and east, who had formerly possessed some part of their grants, before they had surrendered it to the Narragansets, and though they freely owned the submission, yet it was thought best by Mr. Williams, to make them easy by gratuities to the sachem, his counsellors and followers. On the other side, the Narragansets were very numerous, and the natives inhabiting any spot the English sat down upon, or improved, were all to be bought off to their content, and often times were to be paid over and over again.

On the 24th of March, 1637-8, this day an hundred years, the Indian sachems signed the deed or grant of the Island Aquetneck, &c., and the English not only honestly paid the mentioned gratuities to the sachems, but many more to the inhabitants to remove off, as appears by the receipts still extant. And afterwards, at a considerable expense, they purchased quit-claims of the heirs and successors of the sachems; besides, they were forced to buy, over again, several parts of the first grant. So that they came very justly by the soil. And thus they describe themselves, twenty years after, in an address to the supreme authority in England, 1659 : " This poor Colony (say they) mostly consists of a birth and breeding of the Most High. We being an outcast people, formerly from our mother nation, in the Bishops' days, and since from the rest of the New-English over zealous Colonies. Our whole frame, being much like the present frame and constitution of our dearest mother England ; bearing with the several judgments and consciences of each other, in all the towns of the Colony ; which our neighbor Colonies do not ; and which is the only cause of their great offence against us."

The settlement began immediately at the eastward or northward end of the Island, (then called Pocasset,*) round the cove, and the town was laid out at the spring. And many of their friends following them that summer, their number was so

---

* All our histories call the main land, over against the easterly end of the Island, where is now Tiverton, &c., by the name of Pocasset, and in the Indian grant to the first settlers, the same place seems to be called Powacasick. But it is as evident in our records, that the eastern end of the Island is called by the same name ; perhaps if I may be indulged a conjecture, the name properly belonged to the strait in the river or bay, at the eastern end of the Island, where is now Howland's Ferry,

considerably increased that, the next spring, some
of the heads, with others, came to the southern or
western end of the Island.   The Island was divided
into two townships, the eastern part called Portsmouth, and the other Newport; and, 1644, they
named the Island the *Isle of Rhodes*, or *Rhode-
Island.* Thus began the settlement of this Island
and Colony, and through the good hand of our God
upon us, we have continued to this day.   God has
blessed and prospered the people in their labors,
and preserved to them their privileges, for the sake
of which they followed him into the wilderness.

And now, having seen something of the occasion
and manner of our first settlement, let us take a
short view of the history, and present state of the
Colony.

And here, in the first place, as to the inhabiting
the other lands, and erecting the other towns now
within our bounds.—At the same time the Island

---

and the lands on both sides might be called Pocasset, till
the English name of Portsmouth for the easterly end of
the Island prevailed, when the Indian name Pocasset
might become confined to the main land, which was not
settled by the English for many years after.   It is certain,
every remarkable strait, or fall in a river, had a name
among the Indians, as well as every point of land in the
Bay.   A knowledge of the meaning of the Indian words,
would decide all such disputes.

was inhabited, a number of the Providence people, Mr. Arnold, &c., sat down at Patuxet, a place adjoining, and within their grant. They were encouraged by the meadows on the river, which were every where an inducement to people to settle themselves, as they immediately furnished food for their cattle in the winter.

In 1642-3, on the 12th of January, *Shawomet*, or *Mishawomet*, since called Warwick, was purchased of Myantonomy; Pomham, the petty sachem, consenting to the sale or grant, though he afterwards denied it. The grant was made to Randal Holden, John Wickes, Samuel Gorton, John Greene, Francis Weston, Richard Waterman, John Warner, Richard Carder, Samson Shotton, Robert Potter, William Woodeal.

Here it may be proper to take some notice of the religious opinions of Mr. Gorton, whose followers were called Gortonists, or Gortonians, holding some things peculiar to themselves, and different from all the other people in New-England.

He came to Rhode-Island in June, 1638, where he tarried till 1639-40 ; then he was, on some contentions, banished the Island. Thence he went to Providence, where many of the people growing uneasy at his planting and building at Patuxet, and complaining to the Massachusetts Government

12

in 1642, he was summoned to appear before their
court, which he despised. But, however, he purchased this tract of the Indians, and removed there
with his friends. But new complaints soon went
to Boston from some of the English, and Pomham
and Socononoko, petty sachems of the Indians, who
it seems were willing to take advantage of the protection of the Massachusetts English, to revolt
from their subjection to Myantonomy, as Massasoit
had done before, by means of the Plymouth English. Hereupon, Mr. Gorton and his friends being
summoned to court, he refused to obey, as out of
the jurisdiction, both of Boston and Plymouth, who
both sought to stretch their bounds, to have taken
him in. The government at length sent up a company of armed men, who, after a fruitless treaty,
made him and his friends prisoners, except a few
who escaped by flight. They were carried to Boston, and after a trial in their court, condemned to
be confined in a severe, and even a scandalous
manner, in several towns, for the winter, and in
the spring banished the Colony. They came to
Rhode-Island, and fearing to be again troubled,
the Massachusetts seeking a Patent of some of the
Narraganset country, they procured an actual and
solemn submission of the sachems to King Charles,
on the 19th of August, 1644; and Messrs. Gorton,
Greene, and Holden, went to England and obtained an order to be suffered peaceably to possess
their purchase. And the lands forementioned, be-

ing incorporated in the Province* of Providence Plantations, they returned and carried on their improvements, naming their purchase Warwick, in honor to the Earl of Warwick, who gave them his friendly protection.

What Mr. Gorton's religious opinions really were, is now as hard to tell, as it is to understand his most mysterious dialect, for there are sufficient reasons why we ought not and cannot believe, he held all that are confidently fathered upon him. For it is certain, that, whatever impious opinions his adversaries imputed to him, and whatever horrid consequences they drew from the opinions he owned, he ascribed as bad to them, and fixed as dreadful consequences on their tenets; and at the same time, in the most solemn manner, denies and disavows many things they charge him with; above all, when he is charged with denying a future state and the judgment to come, both in theory and in practice, he peremptorily and vehemently denies the charge, and solemnly appeals to God, and all that knew him, of the integrity of his heart and the purity of his hands; and avers, that he always joins eternity with religion, as most essential. And that the doctrine of the general salvationists, was the

---

* They sometimes called themselves the Colony, sometimes the Province of Providence Plantations, and sometimes the Colony or Province.

thing which his soul hated.   (*MS. letter in ans. to Mr. Morton's Memorial.*)

In an address to King Charles II., 1679, he dis-
owns the Puritans, and most unaccountably says,
he sucked in his peculiar tenets " from the breasts
of his mother, the church of England." He strenuously opposed the doctrines of the people called
Quakers. I am informed that he and his followers
maintained a religious meeting, on the first day of
the week, for above sixty years, and that their
worship consisted of prayers to God, of preaching,
or expounding the scriptures, and singing of psalms.
He lived to a great age. He was of a good family
in England, and says he made use of the learned
languages in expounding the scriptures to his
hearers.

About 1642–3, there were two trading houses set
up in the Narraganset country; one by Mr. Wilcox
and Mr. R. Williams, the other by Mr. Richard
Smith, and some few plantations made near them,
on particular grants or purchases of the Indians,
but not very many till 1657 : when several gentlemen on the Island and elsewhere, made a considerable purchase, called the Petaquamscut purchase. And the same year, there was a purchase
of the Island of Canonicut, as the smaller Islands
had been purchased before.

In 1665, Misquamicut was purchased of the Indians, and it was granted a township by the name of Westerly, 1669. In 1672, Manisses, called Block-Island, was made a township, by the name of New-Shoreham. In 1674, the inhabitants at Petaquamscut and parts adjacent, had their lands incorporated a township by the name of Kingston. And, in 1677, the town of East-Greenwich was incorporated, and, 1678, Canonicut Island, or rather Quononoquot, was incorporated a township by the name of James-Town. In 1722, the lands properly called Narraganset, were divided into the two townships of North and South Kingston. In 1729, the whole Colony was divided into three counties, for the ease of the inhabitants. And, 1730, the town of Providence was divided into the four towns of Providence, Smithfield, Glocester, and Scituate; the whole land being filled with inhabitants, partly by the coming in of some few from other places, but chiefly by the natural increase of the first settlers.* In the foresaid year 1730, there was by the King's order, an exact account taken of the number of souls in the Colony,† and they were

---

* In 1738, the town of Westerly is divided, and the easterly part of it erected into a township, by the name of Charlestown, which may be to the honor of King Charles II., who granted us our present Charter.

† The said account was taken before Providence township was divided. The whole account is this:

found to be no less than seventeen thousand nine hundred and thirty-five, of which no more than nine hundred and eighty-five were Indians, and one thousand six hundred and forty-eight negroes. So that the English in all were fifteen thousand three hundred and two.

Some of the principal persons who came at first to this Island, removed again in a little time, some to Long-Island for larger accommodations, some to Massachusetts again, where three* of those families have made a very considerable figure ever since to this day. A considerable number, likewise, removed to the other towns in this Colony, and many settled in the parts adjacent, that are within the Colony of Plymouth. Nevertheless, in 1730, the inhabitants of the whole Island were five

	Whites.	Negroes.	Indians.
Newport,	3843	649	148
Providence,	3707	128	81
Portsmouth,	643	100	70
Warwick,	1028	77	73
Westerly,	1620	56	250
North-Kingston,	1875	165	65
South-Kingston,	965	333	225
East-Greenwich,	1149	40	34
Jamestown,	222	80	19
New-Shoreham,	250	20	20
	15302	1648	985

*Hutchinson, Dummer, Savage.

thousand four hundred and fifty-eight, and of this town four thousand six hundred and forty, who are no doubt by this time increased to five thousand souls. The trade and business of the town at the first, was but very little and inconsiderable, consisting only of a little corn, and pork and tobacco, sent to Boston for a few European and other goods they could not subsist without, and all at the mercy of the traders there, too.* At present, there are above one hundred sail of vessels belonging to this town, besides what belong to the rest of the Colony. God grant, that as we increase in numbers and riches, we may not increase in sin and wickedness; but that we may rather be led, by the divine goodness, to reform whatever may have been amiss or wanting among us.

As to the forms of government we have passed under, it must be observed, the government has been always more or less democratical. At the

---

* Perhaps it may be agreeable to some persons to observe, that about 1660, and many years after, provision pay was one hundred per cent beneath sterling money. In 1687, the prices of goods set to pay taxes in, were, wool eight pence per pound, butter four pence, Indian Corn one shilling and six pence per bushel. If the tax was paid in money, then there was to be an allowance or abatement of one-sixth part, and that perhaps will nearly give the true current price of those kinds of provisions, at that time.

first incorporation on the Island, the people chose a Judge to do justice and judgment, and preserve the public peace ; and towards the latter end of the year, on the second day of the eleventh month, they added three gentlemen as Assistants to him in his office.* And soon after appointed all, to take the oath of allegiance to the King, according to the statute. In 1640, they voted the chief magistrate should be called Governor, the next Deputy Governor, and four gentlemen chosen out of the two towns, Assistants. Their names were W. Coddington, Governor; W. Brenton, Deputy Governor; N. Easton, J. Coggeshall, W. Hutchinson, J. Porter, Assistants. The next year, R. Harding was in Mr. Easton's place, and Mr. W. Baulston in the room of Mr. Hutchinson, (who perhaps removed,) and the next year Mr. Easton was chosen Assistant again, and those six† gentlemen held their offices till the patent of incorporation.

At Providence, all new comers promised " to submit themselves in active or passive obedienec to all such orders and agreements as shall be made for public good of the body, in an orderly way, by

* The three elders were Nicholas Easton, John Coggeshall, and William Brenton.

† The six gentlemen were W. Coddington, Governor, W. Brenton, Deputy Governor, N. Easton, J. Coggeshall, W. Baulston, and J. Porter, Assistants.

major consent of the inhabitants,"* but this being insufficient, 27th day 5th mo., 1640, they did, to the number of near forty persons, combine in a form of civil government, according to a model drawn up by some of themselves, as most suitable to promote peace and order in their present circumstances; which, however, left them in a very feeble condition.

But all the inhabitants in the Narraganset-Bay, being without a patent and any legal authority, 1643, Mr. R. Williams went to England as agent, and, by the help and assistance of Sir Henry Vane, jun., obtained of the Earl of Warwick (appointed by Parliament Governor and Admiral of all the Plantations) and his council, " a free and absolute

---

* The first twelve persons who came to Mr. Williams, and therefore had, by virtue of his conveyance, some prerogative with him, in the divisions, &c., of the land, were William Arnold, John Greene, John Throgmorton, Thomas James, William Harris, Thomas Olney, Richard Waterman, Francis Weston, Ezekiel Holliman, Robert Cole, Stukeley Westcoat, and William Carpenter. Soon after came to them Chad Browne, Wm. Fairfield, J. Warner, E. Angel,† J. Windsor, R. Scott, Wm. Reinolds, Wm. Wickenden, Gregory Dexter, &c. &c., most of whose names remain in a numerous posterity.

† Callender, who is remarkable for his accuracy, here mistakes the Christian name. It should be Thomas Angel. See Backus, vol. 1, p. 74, note.—*Editor*.

Charter of civil incorporation, by the name of the incorporation of Providence Plantations in the Narraganset-Bay in New-England;" empowering them "to rule themselves, and such as should inhabit within their bounds, by such a form of civil government as by the voluntary agreement of all, or the greater part, shall be found most serviceable, in their estate and condition; and to make suitable laws, agreeable to the laws of England, so far as the nature and constitution of the place will admit, &c." It was dated 17th of March, 19th Charles, i. e. 1643–4, but it does not appear how long it was before Mr. Williams brought it over. It is not to be wondered at, if it took them some time to agree in a method.

In 1647, May 19th, a General Assembly of the Province (as then called) established a body of very good and wholesome laws, agreeable to the English statute book; and erected a form of civil government for the administration of the laws, and the making such other, as should be found necessary. The supreme power was left in the body of the people, assembled in an orderly way; a court of Commissioners, consisting of six persons, chosen by each of the four towns of Providence, Portsmouth, Newport, and Warwick, had a legislative authority; at least their acts were to be in force, unless repealed within a limited time by the vote of the major part of the freemen of the Province, to be collected at their respective town meetings appointed for that end.

A President and four Assistants were chosen yearly, to be conservators of the peace, with all civil power, and by a special commission they were judges of the court of trials, assisted by the two wardens or justices of the particular town in which the court sat from time to time.

Every town chose a Council of six persons, to manage their town affairs, and their town court had the trial of small cases, but with an appeal to the court of the President and Assistants.

This form of government subsisted till 1651, when there were some obstructions to it, by a commission granted from the Council of State, to the principal inhabitant of the Island, to govern the Island with a Council chosen by the people, and approved by himself. But the people, thinking it " a violation or encroachment on their liberties and purchases, as granted and secured by Charter," immediately despatched Mr. R. Williams and Mr. J. Clark to England, as their agents; and they easily procured an order from the Council of State to vacate or suspend the commission. This order is dated 2d of October, 1652, but by reason of some misunderstandings between the four towns, it was a year or two before they returned to their old plan, which then lasted to the present Charter.

In 1663, July 8, Charles II. granted an ample Charter, whereby the Province was made " a body corporate and politic, in fact and name, by the name of the Governor and Company of the English Colony of Rhode-Island and Providence Plantations in New-England in America." This *Charter* we enjoy to this day, through the merciful providence of God. And as every one knows the form of government established in it, I need say but little about it. The Governor, the Deputy Governor, and ten Assistants chosen yearly by the freemen, on the first Wednesday in May, have the administration of the government in their hands; and together with thirty-six Deputies,* chosen half yearly by the several towns, make up the General Assembly; which is the highest Court in the Colony, and our Legislature: empowered to make laws as to them shall seem meet, for the good and welfare of the said Company—" so as such laws be not contrary and repugnant unto, but as near as may be, agreeable to the laws of England, considering the nature and constitution of the place and people there."

This Assembly meets twice a year by Charter, on election day, and the last Wednesday of October.

---

* The town of Charlestown being erected since this was prepared for the press, the number of Deputies is now thirty-eight.

The first, by law, is held at Newport, and the last at Providence and South-Kingston alternately. The Governor has no negative voice, and the major vote of the whole Assembly in one House determines in the choice of civil or military officers; but in the passing laws the Assembly sits in two Houses.

It would be too tedious to give a particular account of all the repeated attempts and stratagems made use of, to wrest the jurisdiction and propriety of a considerable part of the lands within our Patent from the Colony.

Therefore I proceed to say,

When Colonel Dudley was appointed President of the Massachusetts, the Narraganset country, called then King's Province, was included in his commission. In 1685, October 6, a writ of *quo warranto* was issued out against the Colony, which was brought here June 26, 1686, by Ed. Randolph, Esq., whereupon the free inhabitants, especially of the chief towns, met at Newport on the 29th, and gave in their opinion to the General Assembly, and left " the further proceeding to the judicious determination of the Assembly." The Assembly, upon serious consideration, published and declared that they determined not to " stand suit with His Majesty, but to proceed, by humble address to His

Majesty to continne their privileges and liberties according to the Charter;" and they accordingly sent home an address to the King, who by his answer promised them protection and favor. However, the Colony was put under the government of Sir Ed. Andross, and " suffered with others, several hardships and severe impositions."

The reasons why the Assembly chose not to stand suit with the King, were partly "their poverty and inability to bear the expense of such a lawsuit in England, and partly the example of the many Corporations in England, which had in the like case surrendered their Charters;" and perhaps the secret hope they should find more favor with the King, by this way of proceeding, was the principal motive.

January 12, 1686–7. Sir Edmund Andross's commission to be Governor of this Colony, with the rest of New-England, was published here, and the Colony made one county, and governed by civil officers under him.

After the revolution in England, there was a General Assembly of the freemen of the Colony at Newport, May 1, 1689, who agreed " that since Sir Ed. Andross was seized and confined with others of his Council (at Boston) and his authority silenced and deposed, it was their duty to lay hold of their former Charter privileges; and avowedly professing all allegiance to the crown of England, they replaced all the general officers that had been displaced three years before. But some of the gentlemen afterwards declining to act by this authority, a General Assembly, called February 20 following, elected others in their room. And there having been no judgment against the Charter, the government allowed of the resuming it, and through the divine goodness, and the clemency, justice, and prudence of our Princes, it has been continued ever since. God grant, we may never forfeit nor lose our precious and invaluable liberties and privileges; and that we may ever use them with prudence and discretion, with gratitude to God, the governor of the world; and with loyalty to the crown!

It is now more than time for me to lay before you, some account of our religious affairs.

It is a pity we cannot entirely confute all the opprobrious things which some have written of some of the inhabitants. I am satisfied a great many of them were wholly groundless, many others very much aggravated and misrepresented, and some things made to be reproaches which in reality were praiseworthy.

I take it to have been no dishonor to the Colony, that Christians, of every denomination, were suffered to lead quiet and peaceable lives, without any fines or punishments for their speculative opinions, or for using those external forms of worship they believed God had appointed, and would accept. Bigots may call this confusion and disorder, and it may be so, according to their poor worldly notions of religion, and the kingdom of Christ. But the pretended order of human authority, assuming the place and prerogatives of Jesus Christ, and trampling on the consciences of his subjects, is, as Mr. R. Williams most justly calls it, "monstrous disorder."

Though it be very certain, that a public worship of God is very necessary, even to civilize mankind, who would be likely to lose all sense of religion without it; yet it will not follow, that the civil magistrate, as such, has authority to appoint the rites of worship, and constrain all his subjects to use them, much less to punish them for using any other. What has been forever the consequences of his pretending to such authority, and using his power to support it? What glory doth it bring to God, and what good can it do to men, to force them to attend a worship they disapprove? It can only make them hypocrites, and God abhors such worshippers.

Notwithstanding our constitution left every one to his own liberty, and his conscience; and notwithstanding the variety of opinions that were entertained, and notwithstanding some may have contracted too great an indifference to any social worship, yet I am well assured there scarce ever was a time, the hundred years past, in which there was not a weekly public worship of God, attended by Christians, on this Island and in the other first towns of the Colony.

It is no ways unlikely, some odd and whimsical opinions may have been broached; the liberty enjoyed here, would tempt persons distressed for their opinions in the neighboring governments, to retire to this Colony as an asylum. It is no ways unlikely, that some persons of a very different genius and spirit from the first settlers, might intrude themselves, and use this liberty as an occasion to the flesh; but the first set of men who came here, were a pious generation, men of virtue and godliness, notwithstanding their tincture of enthusiasm, which was not peculiar to them; and notwithstanding their peculiar opinions of justification, and the nature and rights of the Christian church. They had not so many great and wise men among them, perhaps, as were in some of the other Colonies; but their whole number was very small, in comparison with the other Colonies. Nevertheless, they had some very considerable men, and of superior merit. It is true, likewise, their form of government was too feeble; their first Patent left

14

them without sufficient authority in their civil officers, to check any popular humors; but yet, they did, and that as early as the Massachusetts Colony, form a body of good laws, by which all vice, and every immorality, was discouraged or punished. And throughout the whole history of the Island and Colony, there is manifestly an aim and endeavor to prevent or suppress all disorders and immoralities, and to promote universal peace, virtue, godliness, and charity.

I do not pretend to defend all the opinions that were entertained by any of them; much less, all the extravagant notions that were unjustly ascribed to some of them ; nor yet to justify every word or action that might be the effect of heated zeal, or raised indignation and resentment. That man, who will go about to justify or condemn a party, in the gross, and without distinction, shall never be approved or imitated by me; much less can it be expected, I should defend all the opinions of so many different religious parties, as were here united in civil peace. However, I dare say it after Mr. J. Clark, that "notwithstanding the different consciences and understandings among them, they agreed to maintain civil justice and judgments; neither were there such outrages committed among them, as in other parts of the country were frequently seen." (*Clark's Nar. Introd.*) And I bear them witness, they had a zeal for God: If it were not according to knowledge in ever article, yet they lay open to instruction, desirous to find out and discover the whole mind and will of God ; which cannot so truly be said of all places, where yet men are not more infallible. If there were any of them, who made shipwreck of faith and a good conscience, perhaps it would be as easy, as it would be invidious, to find parallels enough in other places, to shew there are other dangerous rocks, besides liberty of conscience. It is an unaccountable humor that has prevailed among too many Christian sects, to make religion and the gospel consist in their own peculiar and distinguishing tenets, which would almost tempt an impartial man to think it ought rather to consist in those things, wherein they are most generally agreed, and conclude in the words of the excellent Dr. Cotton Mather : " The period hastens for a new reformation, wherein it is likely none of our very best parties will be, in all things, the standard of what shall prevail in the world, but our holy Lord will form a new people of those good men that shall unite in the articles of their goodness, and sweetly bear with one another in their lesser differences." (*Good Men United*, p. 26–7.

It must be a mean, contracted way of thinking, to confine the favor of God and the power of godliness, to one set of speculative opinions, or any particular external forms of worship. How hard must

it be, to imagine all other Christians but ourselves
must be formal and hypocritical, and destitute of
the grace of God, because their education or capacity differs from ours, or that God has given
them more or less light than to us, though we cannot deny, they give the proper evidence of their
fearing God, by their working righteousness; and
shew their love to him, by keeping what they understand he has commanded; and though their faith
in Christ Jesus purifies their hearts, and works by
love, and overcomes the world. It would be hard
to shew, why liberty of conscience, mutual forbearance and good will, why brotherly kindness and
charity, is not as good a center of unity, as a constrained uniformity in external ceremonies, or a
forced subscription to ambiguous articles. Experience has dearly convinced the world, that
unanimity in judgment and affection cannot be
secured by penal laws. Who can tell, why the
unity of the spirit in the bonds of peace, is not
enough for Christians to aim at? And who can
assign a reason, why they may not love one another,
though abounding in their own several senses?
And why, if they live in peace, the God of love and
peace may not be with them?

Indulgence to tender consciences, might be a reproach to the Colony, an hundred years ago, but a
better way of thinking prevails in the Protestant
part of the Christian church at present   It is now

a glory to the Colony, to have avowed such sentiments so long ago, while blindness in this article
happened in other places, and to have led the way
as an example to others, and to have first put the
theory into practice.

Liberty of conscience is more fully established
and enjoyed now, in the other New-English
Colonies; and our mother Kingdom grants a legal
toleration to all peaceable and conscientious dis-
senters from the parliamentary establishment.
Greater light breaking into the world and the
church, and especially all parties by turns expe-
riencing and complaining aloud of the hardships of
constraint, they are come to allow as reasonable to
all others, what they want and challenge for themselves. And there is no other bottom but this to
rest upon, to leave others the liberty we should desire ourselves, the liberty wherewith Christ hath
made them free. This is doing as we would be
done by, the grand rule of justice and equity; this
is leaving the government of the church to Jesus
Christ, the King and head over all things, and
suffering his subjects to obey and serve him.

But to take things in their order, Mr. R. Williams
is said, in a few years after his settling at Providence, to have embraced the opinions of the people
called (by way of reproach) Anabaptists, in respect
to the subject and mode of baptism; and to have

formed a church there, in that way, with the help
of one Mr. Ezekiel Holliman,* and that after a
while he renounced these opinions likewise, and
turned seeker, i. e. to wait for new apostles to restore Christianity. He believed the Christian religion to have been so corrupted and disfigured in
what he called the " apostacy, as that there was
no ministry of an ordinary vocation left in the
church, but prophecy," and that there was need of
a special commission, to restore the modes of posi-
tive worship, according to the original institution.
It does not appear to me, that he had any doubt of
the true mode, and proper subjects of baptism, but

---

* Since this was transcribed for the press, I find some
reasons to suspect, that Mr. Williams did not form a
Church of the *Anabaptists*, and that he never joined with
the Baptist Church there. Only, that he allowed them to
be nearest the scripture rule, and true primitive practice,
as to the mode and subject of baptism. But that he himself waited for new apostles, &c. The most ancient inhabitants now alive, some of them above eighty years old,
who personally knew Mr. Williams, and were well acquainted with many of the original settlers, never heard that
Mr. Williams formed the Baptist Church there, but always understood that Mr. Browne, Mr. Wickenden or
Wiginton, Mr. Dexter, Mr. Olney, Mr. Tillinghast, &c.,
were the first founders of that Church.†

† " I have one of the Century Sermons of Mr. Callender, with a *dele*
upon this note, in his own hand writing." See manuscript materials for
a history of the Baptists, by the Rev. Morgan Edwards, in the cabinet
of the Rhode-Island Historical Society.—*Editor.*

that no man had any authority to revive the practice of the sacred ordinances, without a new and
immediate commission. It is also said, (*Neale,*)
" That his church hereupon crumbled to pieces,
every one following his own fancy, and the worship
of God came to be generally neglected." But I
believe this to be a mistake in fact, for it certainly
appears, there was a flourishing church of the
Baptists there, a few years after the time of the
supposed breaking to pieces; and it is known by
the names of the members, as well as by tradition,
they were some of the first settlers at Providence;
however, it is possible some of his followers might
embrace his new opinions. Mr. Williams used to
uphold a public worship, sometimes, though not
weekly, as many now alive remember, and he used
to go once a month, for many years, to Mr. Smith's
in the Narraganset, for the same end.

There was no reason to lay aside the use of the
sacred institutions of Jesus Christ, because they
had been perverted, for surely the disciples of
Jesus Christ must of necessity have an inherent
right to revive, or rectify, any of his ordinances
that have been misused. The Protestants in
general have done so, by both sacraments, which
they have all of them rescued from some or other
of the corruptions of Popery. And why they may
not be as well rescued from every corruption, as
from some, and why Christians may not revive the

true form of administering baptism, as well as the
supper, is hard to tell, unless we make a charm of
the institution. So long as we have the New Testament, wherein the original commission and instructions are contained, we can want no immediate
warrant to obey the general laws of Christ, any
more than a new revelation, and new miracles, to
justify our believing the old facts and doctrines of
the gospel. The Bible contains the religion of
Christians, and the word of God is a sufficient rule
of faith and worship. Had Mr. Williams adhered
to this maxim, the maxim of the Protestants, and
more especially of the Puritans, he might have
continued an Anabaptist all his days, as it is said
he was more inclinable to them in his latter time.

Bishop Sanderson says, (*Veneer on the thirty-
nine articles*, p. 655,) that " the Rev. Archbishop
Whitgift, and the learned Hooker, men of great
judgment, and famous in their times, did long since
foresee and declare their fear, that if ever Puri-
tanism should prevail among us, it would soon
draw in Anabaptism after it.—This Cartwright
and the Disciplinarians denied, and were offended
at.—But these good men judged right; they considered, only as prudent men, that Anabaptism had
its rise from the same principles the Puritans held,
and its growth from the same course they took ;
together with the natural tendency of their principles and practices toward it; especially that ONE

PRINCIPLE, as it was then by them misunderstood, that the scripture was *adequata agendorum regula*, so as nothing might be lawfully done, without express warrant, either from some command or example therein contained; which clue, if followed as far as it would go, would certainly in time carry them as far as the Anabaptists had then gone."

This I beg leave to look on as a most glorious concession of the most able adversaries. One party contend, that the scripture is the adequate rule of worship, and for the necessity of some command or example there; the other party say this leads to Anabaptism. It seems vey remarkable, that the Puritans, at least some of the Puritans, put the baptism of infants, and the administering baptism by sprinkling, on a different foot from many of the other party. It was one grand reason of the Plymouth people's discontent in Holland, that the Dutch would not reform the custom of baptising indifferently the children of all persons that had been themselves baptised in infancy. And it was once a great complaint against New-England, that the children only of visible church members were admitted to baptism. Nor did the general way of baptising the grand children of the covenant, or the infants of such as do what is called "owning the covenant," (a phrase and way peculiar perhaps to New-England,) take place, without a very great and long struggle : perhaps

15

it does not yet universally prevail. When the first principles and practice of New-England are inquired into, and compared together, and with those that prevailed forty years after; it will be found no great wonder, if a person (and there have been such persons) who heard the unanswerable arguments with which some Pædo-baptists prove the infants of those who are not members of some visible church, are not to be baptised; and the like powerful arguments, with which others prove that other infants have an equal right and claim with the infants of church members; I say, it would be no wonder, if such a person should believe them both, and conclude in the words of the late excellent Dr. C. Mather, on a like occasion, "that regeneration is the thing, without which, a title unto sacraments is not to be pretended; that real regeneration is that which, before God, renders men capable of claiming sacraments; and visible or expressed regeneration, is that which, before men, enables them to make such a claim." *Comp. for Comm.* p. 31.)

But to return. About the year 1653 or 54, there was a division in the Baptist Church, at Providence, about the right of laying on of hands, which some pleaded for as essentially necessary to church communion, and the others would leave indifferent. Hereupon they walked in two churches, one under Mr. C. Browne, Mr. Wickenden, &c., the other under Mr. Thomas Olney ;* but laying on of hands at length generally obtained.

It is remarkable, that the principles of a too rigid separation, planted by Mr. Williams, have taken a deep root, while some other of his darling opinions are almost withered away. That church which was distinguished by holding laying on of hands necessary to all baptised persons, came in time, generally to hold universal redemption.

This Church shot out into divers branches, as the members increased, and the distance of their habitations made it inconvenient to attend the public worship in the town ; several meetings were thereupon fixed at different places, for their ease and accommodation ; and about the time the large township of Providence became divided into four towns, these chapels of ease began to be considered as distinct churches, though all are yet in a union of counsels and interests. And there is a strict Association of all the Baptist Churches in New-England, that hold the doctrine of laying on of hands, in that sense, maintained by yearly meetings of the elders and brethren, at several places,

---

* This last continued till about twenty years since, when becoming destitute of an elder, the members were united with other churches. At present, there is some prospect of their re-establishment in church order.

from time to time, where the affairs of all the Churches are considered.

The people who came to Rhode-Island, who were Puritans of the highest form, had desired and depended on the assistance of Mr. Wheelwright, a famous Congregational minister aforementioned. But he chose to go to Long-Island, where he continued some years. In the mean time, Mr. John Clark, who was a man of letters, carried on a public worship, (as Mr. Brewster did at Plymouth,) at the first coming, till they procured Mr. Lenthal, of Weymouth, who was admitted a freeman here, August 6, 1640. And August 20, Mr. Lenthal was by vote called to keep a public school for the learning of youth, and for his encouragement there was granted to him and his heirs one hundred acres of land, and four more for an house lot; it was also voted, "that one hundred acres should be laid forth, and appropriated for a school, for encouragement of the poorer sort, to train up their youth in learning, and Mr. Robert Lenthal, while he continues to teach school, is to have the benefit thereof." But this gentleman did not tarry here very long: I find him gone to England the next year but one; but there is no reason to think that persons of their zeal should immediately fall into a total neglect of a social worship. One of their first cares, both at Portsmouth and at Newport, was to build a Meeting House, which I suppose was designed for public worship.

It is said that, in 1644, Mr. John Clark and some others formed a Church on the scheme and principles of the Baptists. It is certain that in 1648 there were fifteen members in full communion.* And it is this Church, of which we are, by Divine Providence, the successors, though with some little variation in the points which their adversaries had objected to them, in the other Colony. And thus all the Churches of Christ in New-England have meliorated their opinions, and ways of speaking of some points, since that age of dispute, contention and temptation. However, I have good reason to think, the first founders of this church would have heartily joined in that explanation, which was accepted from Mr. Cotton, by the synod, and which is said "to make an happy conclusion of the whole matter," and I suppose every one of the present members would readily subscribe it, viz. "That we are not married to the Lord Jesus Christ, without faith, giving an actual consent of the soul to it; that effectual calling, and the soul's apprehending by faith, is in the order of nature, before God's act of justification on the soul; and that in the testimony of the Holy Spirit, which is the evidence of our good estate before God, the qualifica-

---

* The names of the males were, John Clark, Mark Lukar, Nathanael West, Wm. Vahan, Thomas Clark, Joseph Clark, John Peckham, John Thorndon. William Weeden, and Samuel Hubbard.

tions of inherent graces, and the fruits thereof, proving the sincerity of our faith, must ever be co-existent, concurrent, and co-apparent, or else the conceived testimony of the Spirit is either a delusion or doubtful?" (*Magnal.* b. 7, p. 17.) In this Church there were several persons, able to speak to the edification of the rest; and I have been informed by tradition, that the greatest part of the inhabitants used to attend this worship, though the members in church fellowship were always but few.

In 1652 (during Mr. Clark's absence in England) some of the brethren embraced the opinion of laying on of hands, as necessary to all baptised persons, and in the year 1654 or 1656, the opinion it was necessary to church communion and fellowship, together with their opinions of the doctrines of grace and free-will, occasioned some of them to separate, and form a Church by themselves, under the leading of Mr. Wm. Vahan; this Church continues to this day, and is numerous; at present under the pastoral care of Messrs. D. Wightman and N. Eyres.

In 1656 or 1657, some of the people called Quakers came to this Colony and Island; and being persecuted and abused in the other Colonies, that, together with the opinions and circumstances of the people here, gave them a very large harvest;

many, and some of the Baptist Church, embraced their doctrines and particular opinions, to which many of their posterity, and others, still adhere.

About 1665, a number of the members of the Church under Mr. J. Clark, removed to the new plantation at Westerly, among whom Mr. John Crandal was a preacher and elder. They afterwards did generally embrace the Seventh-Day Sabbath, and their successors are now a very large and flourishing Church, under the pastoral care of Messrs. J. and J. Maxon, and Mr. William Hiscox.

In 1671, some of the members of Mr. Clark's Church, who had been in the observation of the Seventh-Day Sabbath for some years, thought it proper and necessary to draw off by themselves; and they erected a Church, under the leading of Mr. William Hiscox. It is under the roof of their successors we are now assembled.* Mr. J. Crandal, elder of this Church, died the 12th of September, 1737.

In 1695, several ministers of the Massachusetts Colony came and preached here to some who had desired it. The next year there was a Meeting

---

* While our Church is erecting a new and more convenient Meeting House, we are kindly favored with the use of this, belonging to the Sabbatarian Church.

House erected, in which the public worship of God was maintained by the Rev. Mr. Nathanael Clap. In 1720, there was a Church in the Congregational scheme gathered, and he was ordained the pastor, and is still alive, laboring in the word and doctrine. In 1728, there was another Church formed out of this; the present pastor the Rev. Mr. James Searing.

About 1700, the worship of God, according to the rites of the Church of England, was began to be set up here, by the Society for propagating the gospel in foreign parts. Mr. Lockyer was the first Missionary, succeeded by the Rev. Mr. James Honyman, at present the most ancient Missionary of the Church of England in all America.

So that there are at this time, seven worshipping Assemblies, Churches or Societies, in this town, besides a large one of the people called Quakers, at Portsmouth, the other part of the Island.

I am not able to assign the exact date, when every Church or meeting began, or every Meeting House was built, in all the several towns of the Colony. But there are now in the other eleven towns no less than twenty-five distinct Societies or worshipping Assemblies of Christians; besides several places where there are occasional meetings, in some part of the year, or at certain seasons, as is the custom in the other Colonies, among the new or scattered settlements.

There are in the nine towns on the main land, eight Churches of the people called Baptists, one in every town, except Greenwich, where there is, however, a Meeting House, in which there is a meeting once a month.*

Of the people called Quakers, there are seven Meeting Houses on the main land, and one at James-Town on Conanicut Island; and a constant meeting at Westerly, though no Meeting House yet erected.

There are four Episcopal Churches on the main, one at Providence, to which the Rev. Mr. John Checkley is appointed, and one at North-Kingston, of which the Rev. James M'cSparran, D. D., is the present rector; besides one at Westerly, and one on the edge of Warwick, adjoining to East-Greenwich, which are occasionally supplied by the Missionaries at other towns.

---

* The names of the elders of these Churches are, at Providence, Mr. T. Windsor, and Tho. Burlingham; at Smithfield, Mr. Josias Cooke; at Scituate, Mr. S. Fisk; at Glocester, Mr. Ed. Mitchel; at Warwick, Mr. Manasseh Martyn and Mr. Francis Bates; at N. Kingston, Mr. R. Sweet and Mr. B. Herrington; at S. Kingston, Mr. Daniel Everit.

16

There are three Presbyterian or Congregational Churches, at Providence, South-Kingston and Westerly; each of them supplied at present with a pastor, viz. the Rev. Mr. Josiah Cotton, at Providence; the Rev. Mr. Joseph Torrey, at South-Kingston; and the Rev. Mr. Joseph Park, at Westerly. And at New-Shoreham or Block-Island there is a Meeting House, which is at present supplied with a preacher.

Thus, notwithstanding all the liberty and indulgence here allowed, and notwithstanding the inhabitants have been represented as living without a public worship, and as ungospelized plantations; we see there is some form of godliness every where maintained. God grant the power may always accompany the form, and that all that name the name of Christ may depart from iniquity; may Christ Jesus walk in the midst of his golden candlesticks, and hold the stars in his right hand; and may he heal all divisions among his disciples; may he unite the hearts of all that love him, to love one another; may he grant them to be all like-minded, and may pure religion, and undefiled before God and the Father, thrive and flourish among us!

It remains now that I say a few words relating to the state of the Indians, within the bounds of this Colony, and the circumstances of the English in regard to them.

In general, all the New-English Colonies were at the first but one interest, in relation to the Indians, and though the other four called themselves the united Colonies, there was a commission from this Colony to Mr. Williams and Mr. Clark, to enter into a league offensive and defensive with them.

A few years, three or four, before the English came to Plymouth, the Indians had been dreadfully wasted away by devouring sickness, from Narraganset to Penobscut. So that the living sufficed not to bury the dead, and the ground was covered with their bones in many places. This wonderfully made room for the English at Plymouth and Massachusetts, and those Colonies protected the rest.

In the year 1637, the English with united forces subdued the Pequots, who had attacked their brethren in Connecticut; the Narragansets, who bordered on the Pequot's land, consented and assisted in their destruction, through a desire of revenge, which is remarkable in all the savages, though their old sachem desired to have preserved peace.

The Nanhygansicks, or Narragansets, inhabited the lands, or governed over all the Indians within the bounds of this Colony. They were a numerous, a rich, and powerful people : and though they are, by some, said to have been less fierce and warlike than the Pequots, yet it appears they had lately, before the English came, not only increased their numbers, by receiving many who had fled to them from the devouring sickness or plague in the other parts of the land; but they had enlarged their territories, and that both on the eastern and western boundaries. They were reckoned five thousand fighting men. (*MS. of Mr. R. W. in evidence.*) And Mr. Williams says, they were so populous, that a traveller would meet with a dozen Indian towns in twenty miles.

In the midst of this mighty and haughty people, the little handful of helpless English ventured to sit down; though not without taking all possible precautions, on the one hand, to give them no just offence, and on the other hand to keep themselves in the best posture of defence their circumstances would admit of. But the conquest and utter destruction of the Pequots, had for the present endeared Englishmen to the Narragansets. And the conduct and valor they had shewn, and the wonderful success of their expedition, had made them a terror to all the Indian nations round about.

Mr. Williams at first "made a league of peaceable neighborhood with all the sachems and natives round about;" in this, Rhode-Island was included.

And, on the 7th of July, 1640, Mr. Coddington, with the rest of his Assistants, had a particular treaty of peace and amity with Myantonomy and the rest of the sachems. Nevertheless, the next year there was a misunderstanding, and some hostilities, occasioned, I think, by some of the Indians (if not Myantonomy himself) kindling fire in Mr. Easton's land, Lord's Day, April 4, 1641, whereby an house of his was burnt. But whether it was designedly, or only through carelessness, does not plainly appear in the records. However, it alarmed the people, and among other measures, *they fitted out an armed boat,* to ply round the Island, to keep off the Indians from landing; and it seems, in some scuffle on that account, two Englishmen were wounded, and one Indian slain; though the orders to the soldiers were as mild and prudent as could be given. They likewise appointed garrison houses, to which the people were to repair on an alarm. Among which, I find one was Mr. Lenthal's, the minister. But the rupture lasted not long, before peace was restored.

In 1643, Myantonomy, the great sachem of the Narragansets, was taken prisoner by Uncas, sachem of the Moheags, and some time after slain, and as some of the English say, after quarter and promise of life given. This excited his subjects to revenge his death, but the terror of the English at the Massachusetts kept them quiet. And so it is said, that seven years after, there were some commotions stilled by the same terror, and so likewise in 1653, &c. &c.

In 1652, when the Council of State confirmed their Patent, the people were put on some enterprises against the Dutch at New-York, or New-Netherlands, and the next year the Island sent some men to the assistance of their countrymen, settled at Long-Island, which gave great offence to the towns on the main, and in the two Dutch wars, in King Charles 2d's time, the Colony and Island were put to considerable expense and trouble to put and keep themselves in a posture of defence.

In 1675, Philip, King of the Wampanoags, began a war against Plymouth Colony in June, which soon spread almost throughout all New-England. Tradition says,* "He was forced on by the fury of his young men, sore against his own judgment and inclination ; and that though he foresaw, and fore-

---

* All the histories from Mr. Hubbard and Dr. Mather, make Philip to be the spring and mover of the war ; but there is a constant tradition among the posterity of the people, who lived next to him, and were familiarly conversant with him, as also with the Indians who survived the war, that both Philip and his chief old men were utterly averse to the war, and they shew the spot (Kikemuit spring, in a farm belonging to Stephen Paine, Esq., in Bristol) where Philip received the news of the first En-

told the English would in time by their industry, root out all the Indians, yet he was against making war with them, as what he thought would only hurry on and increase the destruction of his people;" and the event proved he judged right. The Powaws had foretold Philip, no Englishman should ever kill him, which accordingly proved true; he was shot dead by an Indian.*

---

glishmen that were killed, with grief and sorrow, and wept at the news; and that a day or two before the first outrages, he had protected an Englishman the Indians had captivated, rescued him from them, and privately sent him home safe.

* I have heard from some old people, who were familiarly acquainted with the Indians, both before and after the war, that the Powaws had likewise given out another ambiguous oracle, which did very much spirit on the Indians to war at first, and afterwards as much discouraged them, viz. that they promised the Indians would be successful, if the English fired the first gun. It is certain the Indians long delayed, and designedly avoided firing on the English, and seemed to use all possible means to provoke the English to fire first, by rifling their houses, abusing their cattle, threatening and insulting their persons, &c. And the histories carry it, that an Englishman fired the first gun, at Metapoiset garrison, some days before any English were slain. But those ancient people, since dead, told me, that by a mistake, occasioned through the hurry and trepidation which usually attends the beginning of any considerable enterprise, an Indian fired the

When Philip could no longer resist the importunity of his warriors, he, like a wise man, took the most proper measures to make their enterprise effectual, especially by an early endeavor to persuade the other Indian nations into the war, that with united forces they might fall on the English every where at once; and particularly he endeavored to persuade the Narragansets, who had several pretensions to quarrel with the English, and who were then reputed four thousand* fighting

---

first gun, (whether on Pocasset side, where there was a skirmish at the beginning of the war, that is not mentioned by Mr. Hubbard, &c., I cannot now say,) and that the news of this, when known among the Indians, was a fatal wound to their courage, they saying the Englishman's God would now subdue them, which contributed not a little to their after destruction. This I always looked on as a very remarkable passage, but the authors before mentioned, and Col. Church, who had by far the best means to be informed in all circumstances relating to the beginning and progress of the war in this part of the country, being wholly silent about it; and the few ancient people who are now alive, that were actors in the war, not retaining any perfect tradition of the matter, the reader may entertain the story as he pleases ; I dare not warrant the truth of it, but only that I certainly heard the story from some ancient people of Swansey, since deceased.

* Mr. Hubbard says, page 13: "The Narhagansets promised to rise with four thousand in the spring of the year 1676," and in a postscript, says, "Concerning the

men. But whether the war began too soon for them, or the first beginnings discouraged them, or that they did not intend to make war at all; they renewed their league of peace and war with the united Colonies, in July, a month after Philip had began hostilities at Swansey.

However, when he was driven out of his country, they were charged to have received and entertained his people. Whereupon the united Colonies sent an army of a thousand men under Jos. Winslow, Esq He arrived with the Massachusetts and Plymouth forces, the 12th of December, at Major

---

Narhagansets, this is further to be added here, that Mr. Thomas Stanton and his son Robert, who have a long time lived amongst them, and are best acquainted with their language and manners of any in New-England, do affirm that, to their knowledge, the Narhaganset sachems, before the late troubles, had two thousand fighting men under them, and nine hundred arms." These accounts are perhaps both true, for the first might mean to contain all the Indians in the bounds of this Colony, who being under the authority of the great Narhaganset sachem, were often called by this general name; and were perhaps four thousand fighting men. Mr. Stanton might mean only those properly or precisely called Narraganset Indians, in distinction from the Indians at Providence and the Indians at Warwick, who joined in the war under Pomham, &c., and from the Nyhantic Indians, under Ninigret, who did not join in the war; though these were

17

Smith's, in North-Kingston ; on the 18th, the Connecticut men being arrived, the army marched the next day near eighteen miles to a sort of fort, (19th of December,) which the Indians had raised on an Island of upland, in the midst of a most hideous swamp. Their Indian guide led them to the only place where it could be attacked ; the English fell on with too much courage and eagerness, which proved fatal to some of their valiant Captains. However, their victory was complete ; the fort was taken, and it is said seven hundred fighting men, and twenty chief Captains of the enemy were slain that day, besides women and children ; and three hundred more died of their

---

always, and to this day are, frequently included in the general name of Narhaganset Indians. What seems to confirm this, is what Mr. Hubbard adds, viz. " Yet are they so broken and scattered at this day, that there is none of them left on this side the country, unless some few, not exceeding seventy in number, that have sheltered themselves under the inhabitants of Rhode-Island, as a merchant of that place, worthy of credit, lately affirmed to the writer hereof." Those sheltered at the Island were either prisoners of war, or such as had voluntarily surrendered themselves to the English for protection, on promise of life. But it is well known, that Ninigret's men alone vastly exceeded that number ; besides there were divers prisoners at Providence. And that side of the country was much fuller of Indians, in the memory of very many now alive.

wounds afterwards, besides the vast numbers who
perished through cold and hunger. The loss to
the English was of about eighty men; six Captains
slain, and one hundred and fifty men wounded,
many of them by their own friends. Towards
night, they set fire to the fort, and retreated to
their head quarters, through the cold and snow.
Some thought, if they had kept possession of the
fort, where was the Indian provisions, they might
have saved many of their own wounded men, and
that the Indians must all have perished, through
cold and hunger, or surrendered at discretion, the
next morning. Others thought it a merciful providence, they retreated so soon, notwithstanding the
fatigue of such a retreat. But however that be,
which cannot so well be judged of now,* the

---

* Mr. Hubbard represents the burning the fort as necessary to dislodge the Indians, and after that the retreat
must be also necessary. However, he mentions their
want of provisions, by means of their vessels being frozen
in at Cape Cod. He says there was a great quantity of
provisions burned in the four or five hundred wigwams in
the fort. And he several times laments the misery of
the wounded men, in marching near eighteen miles
through the cold and snow that night, before their wounds
could be dressed. But Col. Church, who was present
and wounded in the action, tells us, he vehemently opposed the firing the fort ; that the General was surprised
into it, and he condemns it as a very imprudent and un-
fortunate conduct. He says, " The fort was full of corn

wounded and starving Indians, on their retreat, returned, put out their fires, and sheltered themselves, and found some refreshment among the ashes of the best and strongest fortification the Indians were ever masters of in this country. This was the greatest action ever performed by the New-English Colonies, against the Indians; if we regard either the numbers of men on each side, or the consequences of the action. Beside that, the Indians had now the use of guns, as well as they; and were as expert in the use of them, as any men in the world. The Indians were soon pursued with famine and sickness, so that after they submitted the next year, they were never formidable again. These Narragansets do now in a manner cease to be a people, the few, if any, remaining in the Colony,

---

and other provisions, sufficient to support the whole army till the spring, and there was no other provisions to be depended on; there was good warm lodging for the wounded men, not elsewhere to be had." He supposes every one acquainted with the circumstances of that night's march, deeply laments the misery of the whole army, especially of the wounded and dying men. He adds, " That it mercifully came to pass, that Capt. Andrew Belcher arrived that very night at Mr. Smith's, from Boston, loaden with provisions for the army, who must otherwise have perished for want." (*Church*, p. 16, 17.) Tradition is on the same side, and supposes had the army kept possession of the fort, it must have in a manner finished the war.

being either scattered about where the English will employ them, or sheltered under the successors of Ninigret, a sachem that refused to join in the war, and so has preserved his lands to his posterity; and there are a few Indians now living round him, on his lands, or belonging to his tribe.

As to the part this Colony had in that war, it must be observed that though the Colony was not, as they ought to have been, consulted, yet they not only afforded shelter and protection to the flying English, who deserted from many of the neighboring plantations, in Plymouth Colony, and were received kindly by the inhabitants, and relieved, and allowed to plant the next year on their commons, for their support; but they likewise furnished some of the forces with provisions and transports: and some of their principal gentlemen, as Major Sanford, and Capt. Goulding, were in the action at Mount Hope, as volunteers in Captain Church's Company, when King Philip was slain.*

---

* In the Colony's answer to the King's letter, 1679, inquiring the value of Mount Hope Neck, which was begged of the King, by Johny Crowne, the poet, they say, that "a Rhode-Island Indian, under a Rhode-Island Captain, a volunteer, with a Plymouth Captain, killed King Philip." His name was Alderman, and Col. Church says he deserted the year before, from Weetamore, squaw sachem of Pocasset, and came over to Rhode-Island with his family, and gave good intelligence to the English at that time, which was ill improved or neglected.

The Indians never landed on the Island, in the war time, armed boats being kept plying round, to break their canoes, and prevent their making any attempts. But our settlements on the main suffered very much, both at Petaquamscut, and at Warwick, and at Providence; where the Indians burnt all the ungarrisoned and deserted houses. And the inhabitants made heavy complaints, that when the army of the united Colonies returned home, they did not leave a sufficient number of forces to protect our plantations, which were now, in a very peculiar manner, exposed to an exasperated and desperate enemy.*

---

* I know this was attempted to be excused, by the agents of a neighboring Colony, before the King; and they had the face to assert, that "the Colony would never yield any joint assistance against the common enemy, no, not so much as in their own towns, on the main, nor garrison their own towns of Providence and Warwick, and so that the blame ought to lie on this government, if they suffered spoil, while the army was pursuing the routed enemy." But the printed histories confute this answer in part; the Providence Company, under Capt. Andrew Edmonds, was very helpful, and successful too, against the common enemy, and that even out of our own bounds. (See Hubbard's Narrative of the Troubles with the Indians, p. 28.) (See also Col. Church's History.) I could give several reasons, why the Colony did not act more jointly, and why it ought not to be charged to their fault, that they did not. But perhaps it would be no service to any body now to mention them.

As King Philip had no fortified places, and no magazines, when the foreign succor and assistance, which he depended upon, failed him, when the Narragansets were in his own condition, and the Mohawks refused to assist him, his people lost all hope, and courage, and conduct; being beaten off from their planting and fishing, and pursued by famine and sickness, and divers parties of the

However, I must say, it was not owing only to the religious principles of the gentlemen then at the head of our administration. It is true, the Governor and the Deputy Governor, that year, were both of the people called Quakers, but there are military commissions still in being under their hands and seals, to Mr. B. Arnold, jun., and others, to go in *an armed sloop to visit the garrisons at Providence*, &c. It was but reasonable the united Colonies should have left a sufficient guard, at least, at their own head quarters, and some other places, while the Island, the only part of the Colony able to contribute to the charge of the wars, was at so great an expense in supporting and defending the distressed English, who fled to them from all the adjacent parts. On account of these and some other like aspersions, the forementioned Deputy Governor, in order that things might not be otherwise resented against us than they were, gave an affidavit or evidence on solemn engagement, that " he never was against giving forth any commissions to any, that might have been for the security of the King's interest in this Colony." This, with some commissions actually signed by him, is among a large number of ancient manuscripts in the possession of the Honorable William Coddington, Esq.

English, who had their courage raised in proportion as the other side were discouraged, they were forced to surrender almost at discretion, and beg peace on any terms. Philip himself being slain, and most of the chief captains, the war wholly ceased in this part of the country, and with those nations who first began the war.

Ever since that peace, this Colony has had little or nothing to do with the other Indian wars, but only to assist the other Colonies, when properly consulted and applied to. The Colony bore its part cheerfully in the several expeditions against the French at Port-Royal, and Canada. And divine Providence remarkably succeeded and smiled on the defence and protection of our sea-coasts, which were very much exposed all the two long French wars.

The necessary defence of the inhabitants, was never neglected in the time of war, and, since the peace, the Colony, though so small as it is, hath rebuilt an handsome Fort on an Island that commands the harbor of Newport, and, 1733, furnished it with a number of fine guns, at their own expense. Besides, the Colony always keeps a certain number of smaller carriage guns and small arms, with all necessaries and appurtenances in good order, ready to put on board one or more vessels, as occasion may require, on the very first notice of any enemy on the coasts. And though a large proportion of the inhabitants are not free in their consciences to learn war, yet the military exercises are kept up as in other places, and the success which formerly attended the enterprises of our forces, will, while the memory thereof remains, keep up a military spirit in the body of the people.

The Narragansets, as I observed, were the most populous nation among the Indians, but all attempts to civilize or christianize them were utterly ineffectual. Their sachems would not suffer the gospel to be preached to their subjects, and their subjects obstinately adhered to the traditions and customs of their forefathers. It seems hard that New-England should be complained of and reproached as particularly negligent of the conversion of the Indians, and harder still we should be reproached for neglecting the methods used by the French to make proselytes of their Indians, and most unhappy that such complaints are made by writers that seem otherwise well acquainted with plantation affairs, and are deservedly of great note and character. It is happy, however, these reproaches are not well grounded. New-England, nay, the Massachusetts and Plymouth Colonies alone, have had more real success in the conversion of the Indians, not only than all the larger English Colonies to the southward, but than all the other Christian nations that have settled

throughout the whole Continent of America.   The
sectaries of New-England could never be contented
with such sort of converts as the Roman Catholic
Missionaries boasted of in many places; they had
no satisfaction in the religion of the nominal
Christians in Europe, and thought it would be no
advantage to make such Christians among the Indians, as knew no more of the gospel than to make
the sign of the cross, or who desired baptism only,
for the sake of the new shirt with which their conversion was to be rewarded.   And there was very
great opposition to the making them real Christians.
Their sachems or princes generally, their powaws
or priests always, opposed all their power and all
their arts to prevent the growth of the gospel, as
what they imagined would put an end to their authority, especially that of their priests; and the
customs of the people, their way of life, and their
national vices, made it a most difficult task to
gospelize such people, as must be first civilized or
humanized.   The New-English wonder to hear
themselves reproached, for not intermarrying with
such barbarians, of a complexion so different; they
never had the temptations to the unnatural mixture, as some foreign plantations had, nor do they
know other English plantations used to do so.

As to this Colony in particular; at first, the
Narragansets made it a public interest, to oppose
the propagation of the Christian religion.   And

though Mr. Williams made some laudable attempts to instruct them, yet he was much discouraged, not only by want of a lawful warrant, or an immediate commission to be an apostle to them, but especially by (as he thought) the insuperable difficulty of preaching Christianity to them, in their own language with any propriety, without inspiration. After the war, they were soon reduced to the condition of the laboring poor, without property, hewers of wood and drawers of water; and there is no more reason to expect religion should, by human means, thrive among such people, than among the lazy and abandoned poor in London. The few that have lived much together, on Ninigret's lands, have had several offers of the gospel, as the Narragansets had before; and at present the Congregational minister at Westerly is a missionary to them, and encouraged by an exhibition from the Scotch Society for propagating Christian knowledge, by means of an estate, mortified to them for this end, by the late Dr. Daniel Williams, of London. However, it must be owned we have been too soon discouraged, and too negligent in this affair. Perhaps it is one of the worst effects of the variety of religious opinions among the English, that it has been some hindrance to this good work, and even furnished the Indians sometimes with an excuse or pretence to waive any offers to instruct them. If the manners of any have likewise prejudiced any Indians, it is most lamentable.

The vices of Christians have been an insurmountable obstacle to the progress of Christianity in all the other parts of the world, as there are too many evidences. May these reflections, however, stir us up to adorn our holy religion, and to be careful that we give none offence to any that are without: And may it dispose all persons to contribute all in their power, to further the conversion of these people to the Christian religion. They demand our compassion, and our prayers to the throne of grace, that God would remove the veil from their eyes, and all prejudices from their hearts; that he would convert and save them.

Mr. R. Williams, at first, gave a promising character of the morals of these people; but on longer acquaintance and more experience, he seems to have altered his opinion of them; as appears by some expressions in a manuscript of his, yet remaining. "The distinction of drunken, and sober, honest sachems, is (says he) both lamentable and ridiculous; lamentable, that all Pagans are given to drunkenness; and ridiculous, that those (of whom he was speaking) are excepted. It is (says he) notoriously known, what consciences all Pagans make of lying, stealing, whoring, murdering," &c. 25th 6th m. 1658.

After this account of their morals, I should think it hardly worth while to inquire what was their faith and worship that had so little effect on their conversation, if we had not just heard what a scandal to Christianity the lives of too many Christians are. However, the faith of this people and their idolatrous worship, was much like the other Indian nations. They believed in one great and good god, who lived somewhere at a great distance in the south-west, and that the spirits of good men do after death reside with him. But, the government of the world, they seemed to think, left in the hands of an evil god, the devil, to whom, with many inferior and subordinate deities, they paid their chief worship, at their nicommors, or devilish feasts, as Mr. Williams calls them.

The Indians in this part of America, appear to have been some of the least improved of the human species, without any learning or knowledge in any of the politer arts of life, even without iron and the improvements which depend on that. The strange destruction of this people, now since the wars ceased, and within memory, is very remarkable. Their insuperable aversion to the English industry, and way of life, the alteration from the Indian method of living, their laziness, and their universal love of strong drink, have swept them away, in a wonderful manner. So that there are now above twenty English to one Indian in the Colony. Their few miserable remainders are left, as monuments of the anger of a righteous God, and for our warning and instruction. While the contentions, and mutual animosities of the Indians in general, and their cursed thirst of revenge, made them a prey to the weak, and small number of English, we should learn not to bite and devour one another, lest we be devoured one of another, or of the judgments of God. While we have seen their iniquities prove their ruin, we should learn to break off from our sins by righteousness, and especially abstain from, and watch against the sins, which have been so evidently both the procuring causes and the means of their destruction. When God was conducting the Israelites to the land of Canaan, and driving out the inhabitants, to make room for them, he was pleased to warn and require them, not to defile themselves with the abominations of those nations, lest as the land then spued out its inhabitants, so it should spue out them likewise, when they in like manner defiled it. Though it would be ridiculous to compare ourselves to the Israelites, and the Indians to the Canaanites, in many instances, yet in this respect it may be proper to argue, that if we indianize in our manners and vices, they will in time draw down the like, or as heavy judgments of God, upon us, as those with which he hath destroyed our predecessors. God grant that the people, who have been overthrown in the wilderness may be ensamples to us, to prevent our lusting after any evils, lest we be destroyed likewise of the destroyer!

And this brings me now, at last, to the remarks I promised at the beginning. And

1. The first is, the wonderful and unsearchable providence of God, in the whole affair of driving out the natives, and planting Colonies of Europeans, and churches of Christians, in the place of heathenism and barbarity.

I pretend not to have known the mind of the Lord, or to have been his counsellor, or to be able to comprehend the ways of divine Providence. God's judgments are a great deep, but we must be wilfully blind, if we cannot see that the hand of the Lord hath wrought this.

The discovery and the conquest of America, with the amazing desolations wrought therein, appear a more remarkable event than any other in all prophane history, since the universal deluge. A new world, as it was justly called, discovered to the other, or rather to Europe, and all its riches and glory overturned, and given away to another people, and the aboriginal natives, by famine, sword and pestilence, destroyed and wasted away by millions throughout all America! Who can tell how, or how long it had been inhabited, and by what a series of iniquity, it was ripe for such a fearful desolation, such an utter destruction! If we believe a Providence (and 'tis impossible we can believe none) we must needs think it concerned, in the preservation, and the punishment of kingdoms and nations, and that these parts of the world, though separated, hid and unknown to the rest, are yet as near the omnipresence of God, and as much under his government as any other. And therefore we should take notice of the wonderful providence of God in this great affair. How should we learn to submit our little personal affairs to the Divine Providence, when we see that nations, before Him, are but as the small dust of the balance? And how justly may we say, great and marvellous are thy works, O Lord God Almighty; true and faithful are thy ways, and righteous are thy judgments, thou King of Saints; who shall not fear thee, and glorify thy name, for thou only art holy: Let all nations come and worship before thee, for thy judgments are made manifest. The Most High ruleth in the kingdoms of men, and giveth them to whomsoever he pleaseth.

Again, the settlement of New-England in particular was evidently providential, in many respects. I have mentioned often the prevailing motive with the people, who came first to plant and inhabit in this wilderness; but the difficulties and discouragements in their way were really many and very great, so that whoever reflects the least upon them, "must wonder so many were carried out from a flourishing State, to a wilderness so far distant; for (as one of them, Mr. Shepherd, of Cambridge—his life in the Magnalia—says) they were not all of them rash and weak spirited persons, inconsiderate of what they left behind, and were going to. It was not gain or riches they aimed at. When we look back (says he) and consider what a strange poise of spirit God had laid on many of our hearts, we cannot but wonder at ourselves, that so many, and some so weak and tender, with such cheerfulness and constant resolution, against so many persuasions of friends, and discouragements from the ill reports of the country, and the straits, and wants, and trials of God's people in it, yet should leave our accommodations and comforts, forsake our dearest relations, overlook all the dangers and difficulties of the vast sea, and all this to go into a wilderness, where we could forecast nothing but care and temptations, only in hopes to enjoy Christ in his ordinances, and the fellowship of his people."

Moreover, as these people came not here for plunder, which drew over the Spaniards to the southward, neither did they settle themselves by force or by their own might; but God was pleased to make ready a place prepared as an asylum for them : And since he has wonderfully driven out and consumed the natives by his devouring judgments, their sins have proved their punishment; and their detestable vices have drawn on those mortal sicknesses, which have wasted away all within the English pale, but a few who remain embraced Christianity, or who, by submitting to the English power, remain the memorials of these wonderful events. It is true, the Indian jealousy and revenge prevented a union among their several clans at first, and made them instrumental in the destruction of one another, and the English had great advantages in their arms; but still the Indians vastly out-numbered them; were more able to endure fatigue and hardships, hunger and travel; and were perfectly acquainted with their own country. However, a remarkable interposition of Providence was visible in some of the earliest, and other the most important enterprises against them; and it would be unjust not to give to God the glory due to his name: The Lord is King forever, and the Heathen are perished out of the land! As, therefore, God hath planted this people, and not their own skill or power, so neither let them imagine it was for their merits and deserts. We know not the secret and future designs of Providence. Only let us remember, that He who chastiseth the Heathen, will also correct those who are called by his name, if they turn to folly.

Again. it is remarkable how Divine Providence was pleased to supply their wants in a wilderness, among a people that never took care for the morrow ; and to support them under the distresses

they were tried with. At Plymouth and Charlestown, many died at first, for want of necessaries
and conveniences; but, afterwards, it was many
years before any sickness prevailed amongst the
planters. And though they have often since been
visited with sore calamities, and wasting sicknesses,
yet their numbers have continually increased to a
very great degree; while the natives have been
wasted away by the same diseases, and some other
infectious distempers, from which the English have
been providentially delivered.* I cannot help ob-
serving, here, the very great age to which many of
the first settlers of this Colony lived. Many of
them, through all the difficulties and hardships of
a new plantation, lived here near and some above
forty years, and some above sixty.† Remarkable

---

* Thus I am informed by a worthy gentleman, that an
Indian, coming in from sea, sick of an uncommon fever,
infected his acquaintance, and they propagated the dis-
ease to others, and a very great mortality ensued among
the Indians, in Narhaganset; while the English were
preserved from the infection.

† Many of the original settlers of the Colony, lived
through all the dangers and difficulties of their new settlement, above forty years. Particularly Mr. Wm. Arnold,
Mr. J. Greene, &c., who came up the first year with Mr.
Williams; Mr. Harris, Mr. Olney, &c., who came soon after. Mr. Williams himself lived till about 1682, when he
was buried with all the solemnity the Colony was able to

was the care of Divine Providence in preserving them from famine in a new country, where it was some time before they could be enabled to provide

---

shew. Gov. Arnold, who came up a man grown, the first winter, died a few months before Gov. Coddington in 1678. At Warwick, Mr. Weekes was slain by the Indians, 1675, a very ancient man ; and Mr. Gorton, Mr. Holden, &c., survived the war, and some of them, many years. Particularly Major J. Greene, who came a youth to Providence in 1634–5,* and was a Commissioner for Providence the first Assembly after the Patent in 1647 ; was Deputy Governor of the Colony, 1700, as he had been many times before. Here at Newport, several of those who incorporated themselves, 1637–8, and of those who came to them the summer following, survived the Indian war. Mr. John Clark lived to the 20th of April, 1676. Gov. Brenton died in 1674. Mr. N. Easton, who came, 1638, from Hampton, where he built the first English house, as he did also in 1639 in Newport, lived to 1675, when he died a very ancient man. His son, Mr. John Easton, who, as his father, was divers times Governor of the Colony, died 1705, in his eighty-fifth year. Mr. H. Bull, one of the eighteen that incorporated themselves at the first, was Governor of the Colony after the Revolution. Mr. Ed. Thurston, who was Assistant, 1675, and many times Deputy for Newport, died 1706–7, aged ninety years. Many such instances might be given. And many of the second generation, such, I mean, as were born within the first twenty or twenty-five years, reached

* This date should be 1635–6, or as we should now write 1636. See p. 73, note.—*Editor*.

for their comfortable subsistence. God was pleased to bless their provision, and satisfy his poor with food.*

---

to fourscore, and some to ninety years. If we consider the long lives of so many of the first comers, notwithstanding the hardships and distresses they underwent, and the change of climate, diet, &c., and to this add the great age of many of their children, we cannot call the country unhealthy, or the inhabitants short lived. The proportion of ancient people above seventy years of age, to the whole number of the present inhabitants, compared with the like proportion in other countries, which have been fully settled and inhabited above a thousand years, can be no good rule to judge by. Eighty years ago, the whole number of the inhabitants, and consequently of the births here, was very small, perhaps there were fewer than two hundred families in the whole Colony. And the number of inhabitants in this town has vastly increased the last thirty years. Let me further add, that the foresaid rule will not be applicable to this Colony a great while hence, if ever ; because so many of the natives die in the West-India Islands. It is certain, a very great proportion who die between sixteen and thirty-six, are lost at sea, or die in those Islands, or bring home from thence those diseases which soon prove fatal to them here ; though it is notorious how conducive to the recovery of health, a voyage from those Islands to the northern plantations is generally found, so that we have almost always some or other of their inhabitants here for that end.

* January 22, 1639, it was found that there were but one hundred and eight bushels of corn to supply ninety-six

II. We must remark, (however it will sound in the ears of many) that this Colony was a settlement and plantation for religion and conscience sake. The first comers came on this account; their brethren may have said many hard things of them, in their haste; but it is certain the first planters of this Colony, and Island, fled not from religion, order, or good government, but to have liberty to worship God, and enjoy their own religious opinions and belief. They left England for the same reasons, and with the same views as the rest; and they left the Massachusetts, as they thought, on the like account, and came here to pursue and effect the ends of their first removal into America.

I know well what account the New English historians give of that set of men; but we must remember they were parties, and wrote by way of apology, or to vindicate themselves from the charge of persecution, or error and heresy, both alike odious. Now if it be considered what account contending parties usually give of each other, and in what a light, and with what colors they usually re-

---

persons: which, at the proportion of one bushel and half a peck to each, was not more than sufficient to supply them for six weeks, and yet it was then more than so many months to harvest. But there was plenty of fish, and fowl, and venison; and, soon after, even to this day, all the necessaries of life have been plentiful.

present their adversaries, no one will charge me with any design to reflect on those gentlemen, whose memory is so highly regarded in the other New-English Colonies, if I beg leave to question and suspect the ill character they have fastened on those poor people, some of whom have expressed a deep resentment of the injury and wrong that was done them by the historians of the other party. Whoever considers the character those writers give of all other sects and parties of Christians, and the character some other parties give of them, will be apt to think that both sides are to be read with allowance for their respective prejudices. I say, whoever considers the character the contending parties of Christians almost forever give, not only of each other's tenets or opinions, but of their conduct, especially in so far as relates to the support or spreading their opinions; not only the Papists of the Protestants, but the Protestants of one another, particularly the Lutherans of the Calvinists: (*Hornbeck; Summ.*) Whoever considers how common it is for personal reflections to mix with solemn debates, on the highest and most awful doctrines, as well as the least and most indifferent: I say, whoever considers these things, will readily acknowledge we are not to take the character of any sect or person, barely from the description of known adversaries ; especially when the description doth itself imply many circumstances, which carry the strongest grounds of suspicion with them.

If there be any thing in that observation, " that the nature and import of the questions, about which the difference began, and the zeal wherewith they were handled, intimate something of the holy temper prevailing among the body of the people;" (*Magnalia*) I desire it may be considered, that those persons were in repute with the very best, for holiness and zeal, before this unhappy contention.   Moreover, it must be remembered that the points about which they were charged with error, are of such a nature, as that a person's sentiments may be easily mistaken and misrepresented.   It was long before the Church at Boston could have any evidence of their holding those opinions, which that Church condemned; the witnesses at the last were parties, and transported with zeal.   It is not doubted there was some difference in their opinions, at least in their expressions; but there is much ground to doubt, whether any of them held all the opinions condemned in the synod, and that few of them held many of those harsh consequences which their adversaries drew from their tenets. Besides, much the greater number were never censured at all, but (as I observed before) considered as brethren, long after their coming here.

We cannot reasonably suppose that they directly forgot or neglected the sole end of their removal, but as they followed that church order they judged most agreeable to the will of God, and professed

those opinions and articles of belief they thought
God had revealed, so we must charitably judge, the
life of religion and the love and fear of God did not
go out and vanish away, on their leaving all, for
his namesake and the gospel, i. e. the liberty to
worship Him according to their consciences. And
yet all the other Colonies will be obliged to own,
that the trials and temptations of a wilderness had
some unhappy effects on many who had shewn
great zeal about religion.

However, while we are contemplating the occasion of our settlement, and the ends and views
of our pious ancestors, when we find that religion
and conscience began the Colony, it is natural, it is
necessary to reflect and consider how these ends
are answered by their posterity at present. Our
fathers bore the heat and burden of the day; and
though Providence gave them a pleasant and
fruitful land,* the garden of New-England, yet

---

* Mr. Neale justly observes, (p. 595,) this Island, which
is about fourteen or fifteen miles long, and about four or
five miles broad, (though of unequal breadth,) is deservedly esteemed the Paradise of New-England, for the
fruitfulness of the soil, and the temperateness of the
climate ; that though it be not above sixty-five miles
south of Boston, is a coat warmer in winter, and being
surrounded by the ocean is not so much affected in summer with the hot land breezes, as the towns on the continent." Let me add, we have, all summer, a south or

the subduing and cultivating a wilderness, was a tedious and a laborious business, and necessarily attended with many hardships, straits and difficulties. Their posterity possess the fruit of their labor, and should think themselves obliged to fulfil the pious ends of our plantation. God justly expects that we fear the Lord our God, and love him, and walk in his ways, and serve him with all our heart. It seems that pure religion and true godliness is what we, in a most peculiar manner, owe to God, as the very quit-rents of our lands, and an acknowledgment of the merciful providences in our first settlement; as well as for the constant favors of God to us ever since.

The posterity of a people, who were guided by

---

southwesterly sea breeze, almost every day, which rises about 10 A. M., and wonderfully cools the air. And by reason of southeasterly sea breezes, in the spring, the summer does not come on so quick as at Boston, though the winter usually breaks up sooner.—Here let me be permitted to offer a correction of a vulgar error, about the reason of the cold of New-England winters, which is so very much greater than in the European countries in the same latitudes. The Lakes usually bear the blame of our cold northwest winds, but by a map of the country of the five nations, and of the Lakes, &c., published at New-York by authority, and said to be taken from a map of Louisiana, done by Mr. De Lisle in 1718, it appears that all the Lakes, except the Lake Champlain, are considerably the providence of God to this happy Island, as a safe retreat from the stormy winds, as a place of freedom to practise every branch of religion in, must be inexcusable, if they degenerate and forget the God of their fathers. The very instrument of our original incorporation, obliges us to "serve God and Jesus Christ, and obey all his holy laws." Irreligion, then, and profaneness and immorality, must be a peculiar reproach to such a people. Our fathers will rise up in judgment against, and condemn their degenerate offspring, and the God of our fathers will cast us off forever, if we do not practise that sobriety, righteousness and godliness, which his gospel requires, and we are under so many peculiar obligations to observe. Nay, it will

---

to the westward of the northwest point, from this town. The chief of these vast Lakes are northwest from Pennsylvania, Maryland, and Virginia. All the great Lakes are west from Albany, as the Council of New-York seem to assert; and Albany is, as I suppose, nearer west from Boston than north-west. Besides, it is credibly reported by intelligent persons, most conversant in those regions, that at the most eastern of the Lakes, the winds are usually easterly in those months when we are frozen with north-west winds. Perhaps as our distance from the equator occasions the long draft of winds from north-west, so the vast body of lands, uncultivated, and covered with a perpetual forest, which breaks the rays of the sun, and prevents their reflection from the earth, is what occasions those winds to be so very cold here.

be more tolerable for the Pequots, the Wampanoags, the Narragansets, in the day of judgment,
than for such of us as obey not the gospel of our
Lord Jesus Christ. It is true, the Indian nations
did obstinately refuse the gospel, but they knew
not what they did; they did it ignorantly, and in
unbelief, while we have known our master's will;
and to whom much is given, of them much will be
required. As we have been, as it were, lifted up
to Heaven with privileges, our fall will be so much
the greater in the bottomless pit, unless we lay
hold on eternal life.

If our neighbors observe the manners of the inhabitants are reformed in any instances, formerly
grievous to them, let us endeavor to reform whatever is still really amiss among us, and put away
the evil of our doings, that the Lord God may
dwell among us. May we be noted only, and ever,
for the general discharge of all public and private
virtues, for the impartial administration of justice,
and the steady execution of good and wholesome
laws, and for leading quiet and peaceable lives, in
all godliness and honesty.

It is an old and common observation, that the
stature and complexion* of human creatures, as

---

*In like manner some diseases are peculiar to every
country; perhaps we may this way account for what has

well as of plants and animals, yea, and the genius
and dispositions of a people, are very much in-
fluenced by the soil and climate; by the situation,
the nature and circumstances of the place they inhabit. Thus, the inhabitants of the several parts
of Italy, of Germany, &c., are characterised from
their respective countries; and thus it was observed
of the Carthagenians. The peculiar genius and
dispositions of a people must arise from hence, or
the form of government and laws they live under,
or the genius of the present chief commanders.
The Narragansets, who inhabited this tract of land
before us, were not remarkable among the Indians
for many vices peculiar to them,* only that in proportion to their greater populousness, they exceeded in the vices common to all the Indian nations. Idleness and intemperance are every where
branded as Indian vices; and they were complained of, as shamefully negligent in the education
of their children, and that they had in a manner

---

been, in vain, attempted to be accounted for so many
other ways, viz. the defective teeth so common in New-
England. Mr. R. Williams says, that when he first
came here, the Indians were vastly subject to the tooth-
ach, and that their very stoutest men complained more of
that pain, than their women of the pains of travail.

* Mr. Hubbard says, p. 3: " The Narhagansets were
always more civil and courteous to the English, than any
of the other Indians."

no family government at all. Though the face of
the country is greatly changed by English industry,
and an almost immense labor and expense, yet a
plentiful country will always afford its inhabitants
inducements and temptations to abuse the divine
goodness, and to turn the grace of God into wan-
tonness. If, instead of having been able to teach
the Indians Christian virtues, we should learn and
imitate the Indian vices, how unhappy, how re-
proachful, how lamentable would it be? Surely,
we must think God expects more from us, with all
our advantages of knowledge, with the gospel, the
word of God; which is able to make us wise to
salvation, through faith that is in Christ Jesus.
We have not only the light of reason, brightened
and improved, but revelation, to be as a guide to
us. Let us make the scriptures, then, as a light to
our feet, and a lamp to our path.

And in fine, let every sect and party of Christians
among us, be followers of God as dear children.
Let us be careful to build only gold, silver, precious
stones, on the rock of ages, the true foundation of
our faith and hope. Let us walk worthy of God
to all well pleasing, and adorn the Christian religion in general, in the sight of the Heathen; and
recommend our distinguishing opinions to one
another, by a more exemplary behavior, and
so induce others to glorify God our Heavenly
Father.

III. Liberty of conscience was the basis of this Colony. Our fathers thought it just and necessary to allow each other mutually to worship God as their consciences were respectively persuaded. They thought no man had power over the spirit of God, and that the duty of the magistrate was to leave every one to follow the light of his conscience. They were willing to exhibit to the world, an instance that liberty of conscience was consistent with the public peace, and the flourishing of a civil Commonwealth, as well as that Christianity could subsist without compulsion, and that bearing each other's burdens was the way to fulfil the law of Christ.

I do not know there was ever before, since the world came into the Church, such an instance, as the settlement of this Colony and Island. In other States, the civil magistrate had forever a public driving in the particular schemes of faith, and modes of worship; at least, by negative discouragements, by annexing the rewards of honor and profit to his own opinions; and generally, the subject was bound by penal laws, to believe that set of doctrines, and to worship God in that manner, the magistrate pleased to prescribe. Christian magistrates would unaccountably assume to themselves the same authority in religious affairs, which any of the Kings of Judah, or Israel, exercised, either by usurpation, or by the immediate will and in-

spiration of God, and a great deal more too. As
if the becoming Christian gave the magistrate any
new right or authority over his subjects, or over
the Church of Christ; and as if that because they
submitted personally to the authority and government of Christ in his word, that therefore they
might clothe themselves with his authority; or
rather, take his sceptre out of his hand, and lord it
over God's heritage. It is lamentable that pagans
and infidels allow more liberty to Christians, than
they were wont to allow to one another. It is
evident, the civil magistrate, as such, can have no
authority to decree articles of faith, and to determine modes of worship, and to interpret the laws
of Christ for his subjects, but what must belong to
all magistrates; but no magistrate can have more
authority over conscience, than what is necessary
to preserve the public peace, and that can be only
to prevent one sect from oppressing another, and
to keep the peace between them. Nothing can be
more evidently proved, than " the right of private
judgment for every man, in the affairs of his own
salvation," and that both from the plainest principles of reason, and the plainest declarations of the
scripture. This is the foundation of the Reformation, of the Christian religion, of all religion, which
necessarily implies choice and judgment. But I
need not labor a point, that has been so often
demonstrated so many ways. Indeed, as every
man believes his own opinions the best, because

the truest, and ought charitably to wish all others of the same opinion, it must seem reasonable the magistrate should have a public leading in religious affairs, but as he almost forever exceeds the due bounds, and as error prevails ten times more than truth in the world, the interest of truth and the right of private judgment seem better secured, by a universal toleration that shall suppress all profaneness and immorality, and preserve every party in the free and undisturbed liberty of their consciences, while they continue quiet and dutiful subjects to the State.

Our fathers established a mutual liberty of conscience, when they first incorporated themselves : this they confirmed under their first Patent, and, at the Restoration, they petitioned King Charles II. (*Charter*) "That they might be permitted to hold forth a lively experiment, that a most flourishing civil State may stand, and best be maintained, and that among English subjects, with a full liberty in religious concernments, and that true piety, rightly grounded on gospel principles, will give the best and the greatest security to sovereignty, and will lay in the hearts of men the strongest obligations to true loyalty." And the King was pleased to make them a grant, by which "every person may ever freely and fully have and enjoy his own judgment or conscience in matters of religious concernment, behaving himself peaceably and quietly, and not using this liberty for licentiousness and profaneness, nor to the civil injury or outward disturbance of others." This happy privilege we enjoy to this day, through the divine goodness; and the experiment has fully answered, and even beyond what might have been expected from the first attempt. The civil State has flourished, as well as if secured by ever so many penal laws, and an inquisition to put them in execution. Our civil officers have been chosen out of every religious society,* and the public peace has been as well preserved, and the public councils as well conducted, as we could have expected, had we been assisted by ever so many religious tests.

All profaneness and immorality are punished by the laws made to suppress them; and while these laws are well executed, speculative opinions or

---

*It has been no uncommon sight to see gentlemen of almost every religious persuasion among us, sitting on the same bench of magistrates together. And we may always expect to see it, while that principle prevails, that the surest way to preserve and enjoy our Charter privileges, is so to divide the posts of honor, trust and profit among all persuasions indifferently ; and, in general, to prefer those gentlemen, of whatever religious opinions they are, that are otherwise best qualified to serve the public, and adorn their stations, and to suffer no one religious sect to monopolize the places of power and authority.

modes of worship can never disturb or injure the peace of a State that allows all its subjects an equal liberty of conscience. Indeed, it is not variety of opinions, or separation in worship, that makes disorders and confusions in government. It is the unjust, unnatural, and absurd attempt to force all to be of one opinion, or to feign and dissemble that they are; or the cruel and impious punishing those, who cannot change their opinions without light or reason, and will not dissemble against all reason and conscience. It is the wicked attempt to force men to worship God in a way they believe He hath neither commanded nor will accept; and the restraining them from worshipping Him in a method they think He has instituted and made necessary for them, and in which alone they can be sincere worshippers, and accepted of God; in which alone, they can find comfort and peace of conscience, and approve themselves before God; in which alone, they can be honest men and good Christians. Persecution will ever occasion confusion and disorder, or if every tongue is forced to confess, and every knee to bow to the power of the sword: this itself is the greatest of all disorders, and the worst of confusions in the Kingdom of Christ Jesus.

Liberty of conscience was never more fully enjoyed in any place, than here; and this Colony, with some since formed on the same model, have proved that the terrible fears that barbarity would break in, where no particular forms of worship or discipline are established by the civil power, are really vain and groundless ;* and that Christianity can subsist without a national Church, or visible Head, and without being incorporated into the State. It subsisted so for the first three hundred years; yea, in opposition and defiance to all the powers of hell and earth. And it is amazing to hear those who plead for penal laws, and the magistrate's right and duty to govern the Church of Christ, to hear such persons call those early times the golden age of Christianity.

However, as the best things, the wisest institutions are subject to some inconveniences, while some good may accidentally follow the very worst things in the world, it may be worth our while to consider, whether some inconveniences do not naturally, or have not in fact, followed or attended our constitution. The Popish Inquisition itself, which is such an open tyranny over conscience, and such an absolute destruction of the essentials of Christianity and all true religion, yet keeps up

---

* I am aware some such charges of ignorance and barbarity have been formerly insinuated, and that the people lived in a state of anarchy ; but I hope I have said enough to shew the groundlessness of such reports, which were the effects of prejudice and misinformation.

the face and shew of the greatest decorum, order and harmony imaginable. It ought not to be wondered at, if an unlimited toleration of every doctrine or form of Christian worship, though never so just in itself, and so useful and beneficial in many respects, yet in some other respects may be attended with or productive of some inconveniences. We know some followed on the gospel itself. It cannot be wondered at, if some should make an ill use of this liberty; yea, if this liberty itself should be unhappily a snare to some men. Have never any, in no parts of the Colony, appeared lost and bewildered in a variety of opinions round them? At least, is it not likely there should be some persons so weak and unstable? Have never any pretended to think it needless or endless to search after truth, among so many pretenders to it? And have not some, in the heat and hurry of dispute about the circumstantials of Christianity, the circumstances of order, time, and place, grown cold or negligent about the vitals and essentials of the gospel covenant? Hath not too much zeal about outward things, too often occasioned censoriousness and uncharitableness, and starved the life of religion? Is there no foundation for that character that has been given of too many among us, that "they have a thorough indifference for all that is sacred, being equally careless of outward worship, and of inward principles, whether of faith or practice." And "that they have worn off a serious sense of all religion."

It would be no wonder if some or all these evil consequences should have followed, in some degree; they have often done so in other places, even where there was not the like fair occasion. The tempter always suits his temptations to the circumstances of those he assaults. But these things will be no good objection against liberty of conscience, because infinitely greater evils necessarily follow on persecution for conscience sake.

Nevertheless, our own experience, or the observations and reproaches of others, will dispose us to be peculiarly careful against all these evils, and some others, that our constitution may be peculiarly liable and exposed to. Here in a particular manner, let us be exhorted,

1. To prevent our religious differences from being ever carried into our civil affairs. Let them never make factions in government.

2. Let us study for peace, and to promote mutual love among Christians of every denomination. We should love all of Christ we see in them, and as far as possible speak the same things. On the one hand, we should take heed that charity and mutual forbearance do not sink into lukewarmness and indifference to the truth of the divine institutions; and, on the other hand, we should maintain our own opinions, and manage the defence of them,

when need requires it, with a Christian spirit of candor and moderation. Especially let us be warned by our own history, to take heed of imputing to others, the consequences we think follow from their opinions ; if, on the account of those consequences, we cannot embrace their opinions, yet let us remember every man's opinion must be taken from his own understanding and judgment, and not from the understanding and judgment of other men.

It is no pleasure to any real Christian to see his brethren, the disciples of Jesus Christ, so divided as they are through the world, in their opinions of various articles of his religion ; and much less, to see them so divided in their affections. Indeed, considering the finite capacity, and the corruption of human nature, we ought to expect a variety of opinions in religion, as well as in every thing else. But as the enemies to the cross of Christ make this, though unjustly, a reproach to Christianity, and as many weak persons are carried away with the errors of the wicked, every sincere Christian cannot help wishing that every stumbling block and rock of offence was removed out of the way, and that all Christians walked in the truth with one consent of heart and voice. It is a grief to a Christian, as it is a scandal to the whole world, to see Christians (so called) full of envy and malice, hating and reviling one another, and smiting with the fist of wickedness. This, when all is said and done, is a more full and just argument, that such have no part in Christ, than any supposed orthodoxy of opinion can be of their interest in Him. For by this (says he) shall all men know that ye are my disciples, if ye have love one to another. It is a glorious sight to see the disciples of Jesus live in love and peace, and "sweetly bear with one another in their lesser differences;" to see every one keeping the ordinances, as he thinks Christ has commanded him, and at the same time carefully abstaining from all evil, and the appearances of evil, and practicing whatsoever things are true, honest, just, and pure; whatsoever things are lovely and of good report.

When we have freedom to search the scripture, and liberty to believe, and profess what we find there revealed, how unhappy would it be, if any should neglect their privilege, and be fools and slow of heart to improve the opportunity they enjoy? How unhappy would it be, if any should neglect the worship of God and the institutions of Christ Jesus, because they are not enforced by human penal laws? Let us be all able ever to give an answer to every one that asks us a reason of the hope that is in us, with meekness and fear; and let us lay aside all wrath, anger, malice, bigotry and censoriousness, and endeavor to pay a universal and constant regard to the will of God, revealed in his word. Let us be united to Christ Jesus by a true and living faith, and let every man take heed how he buildeth : Other foundation can no man lay, than that which is laid, viz. the Prophets and Apostles, Jesus Christ himself being the great corner stone. Now if any man build on this foundation, gold, silver, precious stones, wood, hay, stubble; every man's work shall be made manifest. For the day shall declare it, because it shall be revealed by fire, and the fire shall try every man's work, of what sort it is. If any man's work shall be burnt, he shall suffer loss; but he himself shall be saved; yet so, as by fire.

3. Above all things, let us unite in the practice of piety and holiness. Let us do justly, and love mercy, and walk humbly with God ; let us deny all ungodliness, and every worldly lust, and live soberly, righteously, and godly, and perfect holiness in the fear of God. These things we may do without any offence to any party of Christians. If we be followers of that which is good, who are they that will harm us, or be offended at us, on that account. Each party requires all men to be redeemed from a vain conversation; every party owns the necessity, if they differ in the nature of the obligation, of these duties : Let us then unite in the practice of them, and have our conversation as becometh the gospel, which we in common profess. How unhappy, how inexcusable, would it be, if

22

liberty of conscience should degenerate into licentiousness, and open a door for a flood of immoralities ? If, while we plead a right to think and judge for ourselves, and reject all mere human authority in matters of faith and worship, we should neglect the sacred laws of God, and the unalterable and eternal duties of morality ? It is certainly a reproach to Christians, that they can be so zealously affected about the things which are peculiar and distinguishing to each sect respectively, and yet be so cold and negligent of those wherein they all agree. It is reasonable to suppose, those doctrines and duties which all agree in, are the most important and essential. Let us then be truly concerned to glorify and serve God, by a true and spiritual worship, and the virtues of a good life, and to imitate the example which the great author and finisher of our faith hath set us. Let us hold fast the form of sound words we have received, and not make shipwreck of faith and a good conscience.

IV. I hope I shall be excused, if on this occasion I exhort the members of this Church in particular, to review the merciful providences of God, which have hitherto preserved this vine, which we trust his own right hand hath planted. We may sing of judgment and of mercy, in many sore losses and bereavements, in some uncomfortable contentions, and in a total failure of elders, for many years together. Nevertheless, the burning bush has not been consumed; the Church has still subsisted, and been resettled again in peace and comfort. Various are the storms in which this Church has been tossed; but, through them all, God has preserved us. May we, and our successors, be as a name and a praise to Him, throughout all generations! Let us pray the Father of lights, and the Lord of the harvest, to revive and prosper his work in the midst of these years. May He unite our hearts to love Him more, and serve Him better; and to love one another, and strive together to promote his glory, and our mutual edification and growth in grace. May he that ministereth seed to the sower, both minister bread for your food and multiply the seed sown, and increase the fruits of your righteousness.

As this was the first Society settled in church order on this Island, as it is the eldest, (though nearly the least,) let us strive to go before all others in the primitive simplicity, love, integrity, and public spiritedness.

Let us consider, whether we make good the ground of those pious and excellent Christians, who first formed this Church; and whether the successors of men so holy and so zealous, are not obliged in a singular manner to imitate them, wherein they followed Christ. We have professed a subjection to the gospel of Christ; let our lights shine before

men, let us adorn the doctrine of God our Saviour
in all things; and let us hold the beginning of our
confidence steadfast to the end, and let us consider
one another, to provoke unto love and to good
works : In fine, let us contend earnestly for the faith
and order of the gospel, once delivered to the saints;
and, at the same time, maintain the unity of the
spirit in the bonds of peace.   Him that is weak in
the faith receive, but not to doubtful disputations.
And the God of patience and consolation grant us
to be like minded one towards another, according
to Christ Jesus.

V. Is it not proper to remark the very great alteration which the merciful providence of God has
made, in the outward circumstances and accommodations of the inhabitants of the Island and Colony,
since their first settlement here ?

We have reason to think, the very first settlers
did not come here empty handed;* but as their
stock, on which they lived, was by degrees consumed, the produce of wild lands was able to go
but a little way in purchasing a new supply of
many comforts of life ; and they were obliged to
make an hard shift with such things as the present
generation perhaps may too much despise.   I do

---

* Vid. Mr. Cotton's way of Congregational Churches
cleared, p. 61.

not well know how to describe the difference in some articles, in suitable and grave expressions : the mention of some instances would perhaps surprise many.   Let us then be thankful to God, who has blessed the labors of our hands ; and let us not wax fat and kick against God, now we have eaten, and are full of the mercies of the Lord.

Nay, would it be unuseful or improper to think of the outward accommodations which the present English inhabitants enjoy, above the aboriginal natives, and their miserable remainders among us? Doubtless, it would excite our gratitude to God, who has made us to differ, and to say with David, blessed be thou, Lord God of Israel, our father, for ever and ever.   Thine, O Lord, is the greatness, and the power, and the victory, and the majesty, for all that is in the heaven, or in the earth, is thine.   Thine is the kingdom, O Lord, and thou art exalted as head above all.   Both riches and honor come of thee, and thou reignest over all ; and in thine hand is power and might, and in thine hand it is to make great, and to give strength unto all.   Now, therefore, our God, we thank thee, and praise thy glorious name !

VI. Lastly. As the pious people who first planted this Island and Colony, were so concerned about the best way of evidencing a man's good estate, methinks there is no more proper remark for us to finish with, than the duty, the wisdom, and the necessity of every one, to get into a good estate as to God and the future world, and to seek after sufficient and satisfactory evidence thereof.

I mean not to revive the old dispute; I am well satisfied, the difference may be compromised with great ease and justice; but to persuade each of us to think of this article with seriousness, and suitable concern. What will it signify, which of those ways is the most satisfactory, if we ourselves have no grounds for satisfaction, in either of them? And what can excuse us neglecting to work out our salvation, and make our calling and election sure, when God is working in us to will, and to do, of his good pleasure? Alas! how very common is it for persons, who live under the gospel, to be very careless and unconcerned in this matter? for many who call themselves Christians, to presume they are something, when indeed they are nothing? and cry peace, peace to themselves, when they are in the gall of bitterness, and the bonds of iniquity, and have no lot or part in the Christian salvation?

A man's good estate consists in his being reconciled to God through Jesus Christ, who was delivered for our offences, and raised again for our justification. Let us aim to have both the testimony of our own consciences and the spirit of God witnessing together with our spirit, that we are the children of God, and heirs, with Christ, to the inheritance of the saints in light. And may He that is able, keep us from falling, and present us faultless before his presence with exceeding joy.

To conclude, should not this solemnity put us in mind of our mortal, transitory condition, and so stir us up the more to give diligence to make our calling and election sure. The generations of men are passing away continually. Not one person, that we know of, is now alive, of all those who began this settlement, and but few remain of the second generation. Death is daily preying upon us. Should we not then be the more quickened in the securing our eternal welfare ? Should we not do with our might, what our hands find to do, before the night of death overtakes us ?

Let us remember we are strangers and pilgrims here, as were all our fathers; and let us seek after a city which is to come, which hath foundations, whose builder and maker is God. And let us be followers of those who through faith and patience inherit the promises.

Let this occasion, an occasion we can never expect again, excite us to number our days aright, so as to apply our hearts to true wisdom. May we so prepare for death and judgment, and the eternal world, as that an entrance may be at last administered to us into the everlasting Kingdom of our Lord and Saviour Jesus Christ: Which God of his infinite mercy grant through Him: To whom with the Father and the Holy Spirit, be all honor, glory and power, both now and ever.   AMEN.

NOTE.—The Editor has taken the liberty to substitute for the orthography of the original text, the more familiar and intelligible orthography of the present day, and likewise to correct the punctuation, when necessary to render obvious the meaning of the author.

APPENDIX.

No. I.—[p. 54.]

Rev. Thomas Prince, A. M., the author of the work alluded to, page 54, was Pastor of the Old South Church in Boston. He was born at Sandwich, Massachusetts, May 15, 1687, and was graduated at Harvard College, in 1707. He visited England, in 1709, and for several years preached at Combs in Suffolk, where he was earnestly solicited to remain; but his attachment to his native land induced him to return, in 1717. He was ordained as colleague with Dr. Sewall, his classmate, October 1, 1718. He died, October 22, 1758, aged seventy-one. He was eminent as a preacher, and distinguished for his intellectual attainments and Christian virtues. In the opinion of Dr. Chauncey, no one in New-England had more learning, except Cotton Mather. Besides many other works, he published a *Chronological History of New-England*, in the form of annals, 12 mo. 1736, and three numbers of the second volume, in 1755. The value of this book was not sufficiently appreciated at the time of its publication. Mr. Callender, who, in the opinion of the learned Dr. Eliot, was one of the first men of that generation, thus expresses his commendation of this book, in a letter, dated Newport, April 4, 1739.

"It gives me great concern, that Mr. *Prince's* Chronology has been so ill received. I look on it as an honor to the country as well as to the author, and doubt not but posterity will do him justice. But that, you will say, is too late. Some of the very best books have had the same fate in other places and other ages. I need not tell you of Milton, Raleigh, &c. I wish, for *his sake*, he had taken less pains to serve an ungrateful and injudicious age, lest it should discourage his going on with his design. I hope it will not, and hope you will encourage him, for, sooner or later, the country will see the advantage of his work and their obligations to him."

No. II.—[p. 59.]

Ante-Columbian Discoveries.

An Icelandic historian, Torfæus, has claimed for his ancestors the glory of having discovered the new world.* A learned work has recently been

---

* Torfæi Historia Vinlandiæ Antiquæ, Hafniæ, 1705. See Wheaton's History of the Northmen, p. 22–28. Belknap's Am. Biog. 1. 47–58. Examen critique de l' Histoire, &c., par Alexandre de Humbolt.

published by the Royal Society of Northern Antiquaries, at Copenhagen, giving an account of the voyages made to America by the Scandinavian Northmen, during the tenth, eleventh, twelfth, thirteenth and fourteenth centuries. The accounts of these early voyages are published from authentic manuscripts, which date back as far as the *tenth* century. The work is entitled "*Antiquitates Americanæ sive Scriptores Septentrionales Rerum Ante-Columbianarum in America. Hafniæ,* 1837." It is published in the original Icelandic, and is accompanied by a Danish, and also by a complete Latin translation. It is a work of vast labor and research, and is one of the most interesting and valuable publications relative to the history of our country, which has issued from the press. From this work, it appears that the ancient Northmen explored a great extent of the eastern coasts of North America; repeatedly visited many places in Massachusetts and Rhode-Island; fought and traded with the natives; and attempted to establish colonies. The most northerly region was called *Helluland*, (Slateland;) further south *Markland*, (Woodland;) and further south still, *Vinland*, (Vineland,) which is supposed to have extended as far as Massachusetts and Rhode-Island. It is the opinion of the learned and indefatigable editor of the *Antiquitates Americanæ,* Professor C. C. Rafn, and his erudite associate, Professor Finn Magnussen, that the celebrated inscription on the

Dighton Rock was designed as an evidence of the occupancy of the country by the Northmen. This learned and interesting work deserves to be thoroughly studied by every American scholar who feels interested in his country's history.

That Columbus made a voyage to the north of Europe, in 1477, is evident from the following passage, extracted by his son from one of his letters.

"In the year 1477, in February, I navigated one hundred leagues beyond Thule, the southern part of which is seventy-three degrees distant from the equator, and not sixty-three, as some pretend ; neither is it included within the line which includes the west of Ptolemy, but is much more westerly. The English, principally those of Bristol, go with their merchandise to this Island, which is as large as England. When I was there, the sea was not frozen, and the tides were so great as to rise and fall twenty-six fathoms."—*Hist. del Almirante,* C. 4. Vid. Irving's Columbus, vol. 1, p. 44.

The Island above mentioned as Thule, is generally, and, we think with justice, believed to have been Iceland. It appears from the correspondence of Columbus with the learned Paulo Toscanelli, of Florence, which took place in 1474, that he had expressed his intention of seeking a western route to India. We think it highly probable, however, that the knowledge of the previous discoveries of the Scandinavian Northmen, obtained on his visit to Iceland, might have imparted to him a powerful influence in his great enterprise.

That America was discovered by the Northmen, before the time of Columbus, has long been the opinion of many learned men in our country. The following extract is contained in a letter from Dr. Franklin to Mr. Mather, dated London, July 7, 1773.

" You have," says he, " made the most of your argument, to prove that America was known to the ancients. There is another discovery of it, claimed by the Norwegians, which you have not mentioned, unless it be under the words 'of old viewed and observed,' p. 7. About twenty-five years since, Professor Kalm, a learned Swede, was with us in Pennsylvania. He contended that America was discovered by their northern people, long before the time of Columbus; which I doubting, he drew up and gave me, some time after, a note of these discoveries, which I send you enclosed."—*Frank. Works*, vol. 6, p. 77. See also Forster's Hist. of Discoveries in the North. Robertson's Hist. of America.

The learned Dr. Stiles, in his Election Sermon, published in the year 1783, speaks of " the certain colonization" of America " from Norway, A. D. 1001, as well as the certain christianizing of Greenland in the ninth century." As President Stiles was intimate with Dr. Franklin, he had probably seen the work of Torfæus, and the above account by Professor Kalm.

The curious reader will be pleased to see the whole passage in which Dr. Stiles, expresses his views with regard to the peopling of America.

"I rather consider the American Indians as Canaanites of the expulsion of Joshua: some of which in Phœnician ships coasted the Mediterranean to its mouth, as appears from an inscription which they left there. Procopius, who was born in Palestine, a master of the Phœnician and other oriental languages, and the historiographer of the great Belisarius, tells us, that at Tangier he saw and read an inscription upon two marble pillars there, in the ancient Phœnician (not the then modern Punic) letter, " We are they who have fled from the face of Joshua the robber, the son of Nun."*   Bochart and Selden conjecture the very Punic itself.   Plato, Ælian, and Diodorus Siculus narrate voyages into the Atlantic Ocean, thirty days west from the pillars of Hercules, to the Island of Atlas.   This inscription examined by Procopius, suggests that the Canaanites, in coasting along from Tangier, might soon get into the trade winds, and be undesignedly wafted across the Atlantic, land in the tropical regions, and commence the settlements of Mexico and Peru.   Another branch of

---

* Ibi ex albis lapidibus constant COLUMNÆ DUÆ prope magnum fontem erectæ, Phœnicios habentes characteres insculptos, qui Phœnicum lingua sic sonant: NOS II SUMUS QUI PUGERUNT A FACIE JOSHUÆ FRÆDONIS FILII NUN.—Evag. hist. ecc. l. 4, c. 18. Procop. Vandalic. l. 2.

the Canaanitish expulsions might take the resolution of the ten tribes, and travel north-eastward to where never man dwelt, become the Tchuschi and Tungusi Tartars about Kamschatka and Tscukotskoinoss in the north-east of Asia: thence, by water, passing over from island to island through the northern Archipelago to America, become the scattered Sachemdoms of these northern regions. It is now known that Asia is separated by water from America, as certainly appears from the Baron Dulfeldt's voyage round the north of Europe into the Pacific Ocean, A. D. 1769. Amidst all the variety of national dialects, there reigns a similitude in their language, as there is also in complexion and beardless features, from Greenland to Del Fuego, and from the Antilles to Otaheite, which shew them to be one people.

" A few scattered accounts, collected and combined together, may lead us to two certain conclusions, 1. That all the American Indians are one kind of people. 2. That they are the same as the people in the north-east of Asia.

" An Asiatic territory, three thousand miles long and fifteen hundred wide, above the 40th degree of latitude, to the Hyperborean ocean, contains only one million of souls settled as our Indians ; as appears from the numerations and estimates collected by M. Muller, and other Russian Academicians in 1769. The Koreki, Jakuhti and Tungusii living on the eastern part of this territory next to America, are naturally almost beardless, like the Samoieds in Siberia, the Ostiacs and Calmuks, as well as the American Indians : all these having also the same custom of plucking out the few hairs of very thin beards.

They have more similar usages and fewer dissimilar ones, than the Arabians of the Koreish tribe, and Jews who sprang from Abraham : or than those that subsist among the European nations, who sprang from one ancestor; or those Asiatic nations, which sprang from Shem. The portrait painter, Mr. Smibert, who accompanied Dr. Berkeley, then Dean of Derry, and afterward Bishop of Cloyne, from Italy to America in 1728, was employed by the grand Duke of Tuscany, while at Florence, to paint two or three Siberian Tartars, presented to the Duke by the Czar of Russia. This Mr. Smibert, upon his landing at Narraganset Bay with Dr. Berkeley, instantly recognized the Indians here to be the same people as the Siberian Tartars whose pictures he had taken. Moravian Indians, from Greenland and South-America, have met those in our latitude at Bethlehem, and have been clearly perceived to be the same people. The Kamschatdale Tartars have been carried over from Asia to America, and compared with our Indians, and found to be the same people. These Asiatic Tartars, from whom the American aboriginals derived, are distinct from, and far less numerous than, the Mongul and other Tartars which, for ages, under Tamerlane and other chieftains, have deluged and over-ran the southern ancient Asiatic empires. Attending to the rational and just deductions, from these and other disconnected data combined together, we may perceive, that all the Americans are one people—that they came hither certainly from the north-east of Asia ; probably also from the Mediterranean ; and, if so, that they are Canaanites, though arriving hither by different routes. The ocean current from the north of Asia might waft the beardless Samoieds or Tchuschi from the mouth of Jenesea or the Oby, around Nova Zembla to Greenland, and thence to Labrador, many ages after the refugees from Joshua might have colonized the tropical regions. Thus Providence might have ordered three divisions of the same people from different parts of the world, and perhaps in very distant ages, to meet together on this continent, or 'our Island,' as the six nations call it, to settle different parts of it, many ages before the present accession of Japhet, or the former visitation of Madoc, 1001, or the certain colonization from Norway, A. D. 1001, as well as the certain christianizing of Greenland in the ninth century ; not to mention the visit of still greater antiquity by the Phœnicians, who charged the Dighton rock and other rocks in Narraganset Bay with Punic inscriptions, remaining to this day. Which last I myself have repeatedly seen and taken off at large, as did Professor Sewall."— *President Stiles's Election Sermon, preached before the General Assembly of the State of Connecticut, at Hartford*, May 8, 1783, p. 10–13.

In confirmation of Dr. Stiles' views, it may be remarked that the aborigines of our country resemble the Asiatics, especially the *Tartars*, more than the inhabitants of any other part of the world. They have the same prominency of the cheek bones—their faces are broad at the forehead and narrowing to the chin. Both the Indians and the Tartars are accustomed to shave the head, and to leave only one tuft of hair to grow on the back of the skull. Both also worship the sun as a deity. We find that the aborigines were here when the

Scandinavian Northmen first landed on our shores; but the narratives of their voyages give no information concerning their origin.

As President Stiles was for more than twenty years a resident and a distinguished ornament of Rhode-Island, a short biographical notice of him is here subjoined.

—

EZRA STILES, D. D., LL. D., was the son of the Rev. Isaac Stiles, of North-Haven, Connecticut, and was born December 10, 1727. He graduated at Yale College in 1746, with the reputation of being one of the most accomplished scholars it had ever produced. In 1749, he was chosen one of its tutors, and in that station he remained six years. He was ordained pastor of the second Congregational Church, in Newport, R. I., the 22d of October, 1755, and continued the able, devoted, and highly esteemed minister of that Church, till he was elected President of Yale College, in 1777. He presided over that institution, with distinguished ability, till his death, May 12, 1795, in the sixty-eighth year of his age. President Stiles was one of the most learned men that our country has ever produced. As a scholar, he was familiar with every department of learning. He had a profound and critical knowledge of the Latin, Greek, French and

Hebrew languages; in the Samaritan, Chaldee, Syriac and Arabic he had made considerable progress; and he had bestowed some attention on the Persic and Coptic. He had a passion for history, and an intimate acquaintance with the rabbinical writings and with those of the fathers of the Christian Church. Dr. Stiles maintained an extensive literary correspondence with many eminent persons in remote quarters of the globe; and his name was enrolled as a member of several learned societies in his own and in foreign countries. As a preacher, he was impressive and eloquent; and the excellence of his sermons was enhanced by the energy of his delivery, and by the unction which pervaded them. His catholic spirit embraced good men of every nation, sect, and party. In the cause of civil and religious liberty he was enthusiastic. In his discourse on Christian Union, he says, "There ought to be no restrictions on the conscience of an honest and sober believer of revelation. The right of conscience and of private judgment is unalienable; and it is truly the interest of all mankind to unite themselves into one body, for the liberty, free exercise and unmolested enjoyment of this right, especially in religion. Not all the difference of sentiment, not all the erroneous opinions that have yet been started, afford just umbrage for its extinction, abridgement or embarrassment." p. 28.

The following appropriate remarks are from the pen of Chancellor Kent, one of Dr. Stiles' pupils.

"President Stiles's zeal for civil and religious liberty, was kindled at the altar of the English and New-England Puritans, and it was animating and vivid. A more constant and devoted friend to the Revolution and Independence of this country, never existed. He had anticipated it as early as the year 1760, and his whole soul was enlisted in favor of every measure which led on gradually to the formation and establishment of the American Union. The frequent appeals he was accustomed to make to the heads and hearts of his pupils, concerning the slippery paths of youth; the grave duties of life; the responsibilities of man; and the perils, and hopes, and honors, and destiny of our country, will never be forgotten by those who heard them; and especially when he came to touch, as he often did, with 'a master's hand and prophet's fire' on the bright vision of the future prosperity and splendor of the United States. Take him for all in all, this extraordinary man was undoubtedly one of the purest and best gifted men of his age. In addition to his other eminent attainments, he was clothed with humility, with tenderness of heart, with disinterested kindness, and with the most artless simplicity. He was distinguished for the dignity of his deportment, the politeness of his address, and the urbanity of his manners. Though he was uncompromising in his belief and vindication of the great fundamental doctrines of the Protestant faith, he was nevertheless of the most catholic and charitable temper, resulting equally from the benevolence of his disposition and the spirit of the gospel."—*Kent's Address delivered at New-Haven, before the Phi Beta Kappa Society,* 1831. See Holmes's Life of President Stiles.

No. III.—[p. 59.]

Voyage of Verrazzano to America.

January 17, 1524, Giovanni Verrazzano, a Florentine, in the service of Francis I., King of France, sailed from a desert rock near the Island of Madeira, in the ship Dolphin, to make discovery of new countries. He steered a westerly course, and, after encountering a violent tempest on the 24th of February, he arrived, about the middle of March, on the American coast, in latitude thirty-four degrees north, probably near that part of North Carolina on which Wilmington now stands. He pursued his voyage northwesterly to the shores of New-Jersey. The harbor of New-York attracted his notice for its convenience and pleasantness. Afterwards, pursuing his course eastward, he passed Block-Island, which struck him by its resemblance to the Island of Rhodes. Fifteen leagues more brought him to the spacious haven of Newport, where he remained for more than fifteen days. The natives " were the most beautiful and well behaved people he had met with in all his voyage." On the 6th of May, leaving the waters of Rhode-

Island, the intrepid navigator sailed along the coast of New-England to Nova Scotia, till within nearly the fiftieth degree of northern latitude. See an able article in the North American Review, vol. 45, p. 293. *" The Life and Voyages of Verrazzano,"* *by George W. Greene, Esq., U. S. Consul at Rome.* Il Capitano Giovanni da Verrazzano Fiorentino di Normandia alla Serenissima Corona d' Francia. Diepa a di 8 d'Luglio 1524. Lettera di Ferdinando Carli a suo Padre a Firenze. These letters have been copied by Mr. Greene, and presented to the Rhode-Island Historical Society. Hakluyt's Voyages, vol. 2, p. 295–300.

No. IV.—[p. 79.]

Roger Williams* was the first person in modern Christendom to maintain the doctrine of religious liberty and unlimited toleration. His "Bloody Tenent of Persecution for cause of conscience, discussed between Truth and Peace," &c. &c., was

* For an able and interesting delineation of the life and character of this extraordinary man, whose name deserves to be enrolled with the legislators of ancient times, or with the statesmen of modern Europe, see a "Memoir of Roger Williams," by the Rev. Professor Knowles, of the Theological Institution at Newton, Massachusetts; see also "Whatcheer, or Roger Williams in Banishment." A Poem, by the Hon. Job Durfee, Chief Justice of the State of Rhode-Island.

published in London in 1644. It is a small quarto, of two hundred and forty-seven pages. In this work he maintains the absolute right of every man, to a "full liberty in religious concernments," supported by the most luminous and powerful reasoning. Here are disclosed principles, which have excited admiration in the writings of Jeremy Taylor, Milton, Locke and Furneau. A reply was written by Mr. Cotton, an eminent clergyman in Boston, and printed in London in 1647. Mr. Williams published a rejoinder, entitled " The Bloody Tenent, yet more Bloody by Mr. Cotton's endeavor to wash it white in the Blood of the Lamb. Of whose precious Blood, spilt in the Blood of his servants ; and of the blood of millions spilt in former and later wars for conscience sake, that most Bloody Tenent of Persecution for cause of conscience, upon a second trial, is found now more apparently and more notoriously guilty. In this rejoinder to Mr. Cotton, are principally, I. The Nature of Persecution. II. The Power of the civil Sword in Spirituals, examined. III. The Parliament's permission of Dissenting Consciences, justified. Also (as a Testimony to Mr. Clark's Narrative) is added a letter to Mr. Endicot, Governor of the Massachusetts, in N. E. By R. Williams, of Providence in New-England. London, printed for Giles Calvert, and are to be sold at the black-spread-Eagle at the West-end of Pauls, 1652." It is a quarto volume of three hundred and seventy-four pages. The

same clear, enlarged and consistent views of religious freedom are maintained in this last work, as
in his preceding, with additional arguments, evinc-
ing an acute, vigorous, and fearless mind, imbued
with various erudition and undissembled piety.

In an appendix is the following address :

" To the Clergy of the four great Parties, professing the
     name of Christ Jesus, in England, Scotland, and Ireland,
     viz. the Popish, Prelatical, Presbyterian, and Inde-
     pendent.

Worthy Sirs—I have pleaded the cause of your several
and respective consciences, against the bloody doctrine of
persecution, in my former labors, and in this my present
rejoinder to Mr. Cotton.

And yet I must pray leave without offence to say, I
have impartially opposed and charged your consciences
also, so far as guilty of that bloody doctrine of persecuting
each other for your consciences.

You four have torn the seamless coat of the Son of
God into four pieces, and, to say nothing of former times
and tearings, you four have torn the three nations into
thousands of pieces and distractions.

The two former of you, the Popish and Protestant Prelatical, are brethren: so are the latter, the Presbyterian
and Independent. But, oh, how *rara est*, &c ? What
concord, what love, what pity, hath ever yet appeared

amongst you, when the providence of the Most High and only wise hath granted you your patents of mutual and successive dominion and precedency?

Just like two men, whom I have known break out to blows and wrestling, so have the Protestant Bishops fought and wrestled with the Popish, and the Popish with the Protestant! The Presbyterian with the Independent, and the Independent with the Presbyterian! And our chronicles and experiences have told this nation, and the world, how he whose turn it is to be brought under, hath ever felt an heavy wrathful hand of an unbrotherly and unchristian persecutor.

Meanwhile, what outcries for a sword, a sword at any price, on any terms, wherewith to take final revenges on such their blasphemous and heretical adversaries and cor-rivals?

Hence is it, that the magistrate hath been so courted, his person adored and deified, and his religion magnified and exalted.

Amongst the people, some have thought and said, how hath the shining of the magistrate's money and sword out-shined the nobility of his person, or the Christianity of his conscience? For when the person changes and re-ligion too, how grossly notorious have been the Clergy's changes also? For instance, how have they pernified, tacked and turned about, (as the wind hath blown,) from Popery to Protestantism, from Protestantism to Popery, and from Popery to Protestantism again, and this within the compass of about a dozen years ; as the purse and sword-bearers were changed, whatever the persons of those Princes (male or female, men or children, or their consciences, Popish or Protestant) were.

Yea, how justly in the late King's book (if his) are the Clergy of England charged with horrible breach of vows and oaths of canonical obedience to their fathers the Bishops, against whom, in the turn of the times and the sword-bearers, they turned to the Scotch Presbyters, their fathers' dreadful enemies and persecutors ?

Now as to the persecuting each of other, I confess the wolf, (the persecutor,) devours the goat, the swine, yea the very fox, and other creatures, as well as the inoffensive sheep and lamb. Yet, as the Lord Jesus made use of that excellent fable or similitude of a wolf getting on a sheep's-skin, so may I not unseasonably make use of that of the wolf and the poor lamb coming down to drink upon the same brook and stream together. The wolf, cruel and strong, drinks above and aloft : the lamb, innocent and weak, drinks upon the stream below. The wolf questions and quarrels the lamb for corrupting and defiling the waters. The lamb, not daring to plead how easily the wolf, drinking higher, might transfer defilement downward, but pleads improbability and impossibility, that the waters descending could convey defilement upwards. This is the controversy, this the plea. But who shall judge ? Be the lamb never so innocent, his plea never so just, his adversary the wolf will be his judge, and being so cruel and so strong, soon tears the lamb in pieces.

Thus the cruel beast, armed with the power of the Kings, (Revel. 17) sits judge in his own quarrels against the lamb, about the drinking at the waters. And thus, saith Mr. Cotton, the judgment ought to pass upon the heretic, not for matter of conscience, but for sinning against his conscience.

Object. Methinks I hear the great charge against the Independent party to be the great pleaders for liberty of conscience, &c.

Answer. Oh the horrible deceit of the hearts of the sons of men! And what excellent physic can we prescribe to others, till our soul, as Job said, come to be in their soul's cases? What need have we to be more vile (with Job) before God, to walk in holy sense of self-insufficiency, to cry for the blessed leadings of the holy spirit of God, to guide and lead our heads and hearts uprightly?

For, to draw the curtain and let in the light a little, do not all persecutors themselves zealously plead for freedom, for liberty, for mercy to men's consciences, when themselves are in the grates, and pits, and under hatches?

Doth not Gesner tell us of a gentleman in Germany, who, fitting his pitfall for wild beasts, found in the morning a woman, a wolf, and a fox in three several corners, as full of fear, and as quiet, and desirous of liberty, one as well as another?

Thus bloody Gardiner and Bonner, (prisoners during King Edward's days,) yea, and that bloody Queen Mary herself, all plead the freedom of their consciences. What most humble supplications, and indeed unanswerable arguments for liberty of conscience, have the Papists, when in restraint, presented, and especially in King James's time ? Yea, what excellent subscriptions to this soul-freedom are interwoven in many passages of the late King's book, if his ? Yea, and one of his chaplains, so called, Doctor Jer. Taylor, what an everlasting monumental testimony did he publish to this truth, in that his excellent discourse, of the liberty of prophecying ? Yea, the formerly non-conforming Presbyterian and Independent, Scotch and English, old and new, what most humble and pious addresses have they made before the whole world, to Princes and Parliaments, for just mercy, in true petitions of right, to their consciences ? But, let this present discourse, and Mr. Cotton's fig-leaf evasions and distinctions ; let the practices of the Massachusetts in New-England, in twenty years persecution ; and this last of Mr. Clarke, Obadiah Holmes, and others, be examined. Yea, let the Independent minister's late proposals be weighed with the double weight of God's sanctuary, and it will appear what mercy the poor souls of all men, and Jesus Christ in any of them, may expect from the very Independent's Clergy themselves.

Object. But doth not their proposals provide a liberty to such as fear God, viz. that they may freely preach without an ordination ! and that such as are not free to the public assemblies, may have liberty to meet in private.

Answer. It may so please the father of lights to shew them that their lines and models, and New-England's copy also, after which they write and pencil, are but more and more refined images, whereby to worship the invisible God : and that still, as before, the wolf (the persecutor) must judge of the lamb's drinking !

For instance, New England's laws, lately published in Mr. Clark's Narrative, tell us how free it shall be for people to gather themselves into church-estate ; how free to choose their own ministers ; how free to enjoy all the ordinances of Christ Jesus, &c. But yet, provided, so and so, upon the point, that the civil state must judge of the spiritual, to wit : whether persons be fit for church-estate, whether the gathering be right, whether the people's choice be right, doctrines right, and what is this in truth, but to swear that blasphemous oath of supremacy again, to the Kings, and Queens, and Magistrates of this and other nations, instead of the Pope, &c. ?

Into these prisons and cages, do those otherwise worthy and excellent men, the Independents, put all the children of God, and all the children of men in the whole world, and then bid them fly and walk at liberty, (to wit, within the conjured circle,) so far as they please.

To particularize briefly : when they have in their six several circuits, ejected, according to their proposals, it may be hundreds, it may be thousands, if impartial of Episcopal and Presbyterian Ministers, and that without and against their people's consent, to the present distressing of thousands, and enraging, through such soul-oppressions, the whole nation ! Then, say they, it shall be free for all that be able, &c., to be preachers, though not ordained, &c. But, provided, that two ministers' hands, at least, which upon the point, is instead of an ordination, be to their approbation, &c. Upon this lock, any shall be free to preach Christ Jesus, upon this point of the compass, as I may in humble reverence, and with sorrow speak it, the spirit of God shall be free to breathe and operate in the souls of men! By this plummet, and line, rule, and square, and, seeming, golden reed, and metewand, the sanctuary must be built and measured, &c.

But further, if any shall be of tender consciences, and that the common size will not serve their foot, if they shall think the Independent's foundations too weak, or it may be too strong for their weak belief, if they cannot bow down to their golden image, though of the finest and latest edition and fashion; why God forbid they should be forced to church as others, they shall enjoy their liberty, and meet apart in private. But, provided they acquaint the civil magistrate, that is, as it may fall out, (who knows how soon?) and too often hath fallen out, the poor sheep and deer of Christ must take license of and betray themselves unto the paws and jaws of their lion-like persecutors.

Hear O Heavens, give ear O Earth! What is this but like the treacherous Dutchmen, who capitulate of leagues of peace and amity with their neighbor English, and in the midst of State compliments, some say out of malicious wrath, others say it was out of drunken intoxications at the best, thunder out broadsides of fire and smoke of per-
cution?

Object. Some possibly may say, Your just suffering from the Independents in New-England makes you speak revenges against them in old.

Answer. What I have suffered in my estate, body, name, spirit, I hope through help from Christ, and for his sake I have desired to bear with a spirit of patience and of respect and love, even to my persecutors. As to particulars, I have and must, if God so will, further debate them with my truly honored and beloved adversary, Mr. Cotton.

But as to you, worthy Sirs, men of learning and men of personal holiness, many of you, I truly desire to be far from envying your honors, pleasures, and revenues, from whence the two former Popish and Prelatical are ejected, unto which the two later Presbyterian and Independent are advanced. Nor would I move a tongue or pen that any of you now possessed, should be removed or disturbed, until your consciences by the holy spirit of God, or the consciences of the people, to whom you serve or minister, shall be otherwise, than as you are yet, persuaded.

Much rather would I make another humble plea, and that I believe with all the reason and justice in the world, that such who are ejected, undone, impoverished, might some way from the State or you receive relief and succor: considering, that the very nation's constitution hath occasioned parents to train up, and persons to give themselves to studies, though in truth but in a way of trade and bargaining before God, yet, it is according to the custom of the nation, who ought therefore to share also in the fault of such priests and ministers who in all changes are ejected.

I end with humble begging to the Father of Spirits, to persuade and possess yours with a true sense of three particulars.

First, Of the yokes of soul-oppression, which lie upon the necks of most of the inhabitants of the three nations, and of the whole world; as if Cham's curse from Noah were upon them, servants of servants as they are, and that in the matters of the soul's affection unto God, which call for the purest liberty. I confess the world lies in wickedness, and loveth darkness more than light; but why should you help on those yokes, and force them to receive a doctrine, to pray, to give thanks, &c., without an heart? Yea, and, in the many changes and cases incident, against their heart and soul's consent?

Secondly, Of the bloodiness of that most bloody doctrine of persecution for cause of conscience, with all the winding stairs and back doors of it, &c. Some professors, true and false, sheep and goats, are daily found to differ in their apprehensions, persuasions, professions, and that to bonds and death.

What now, shall these be wracked, their souls, their bodies, their purses, &c? Yea, if they refuse, deny, oppose the doctrine of Christ Jesus, whether Jews or Gentiles, why should you call for fire from Heaven, which suits not with Christ Jesus, his spirit or ends? Why should you compel them to come in, with any other sword but that of the spirit of God, who alone persuaded Japhet to come into the tents of Shem, and can in his holy season prevail with Shem to come into the tents of Japhet?

Thirdly, Of that bias of self-love which hails and sways our minds to hold so fast this bloody Tenent. You know it is the spirit of love from Christ Jesus, that turns our feet from the tradition of fathers, &c. That sets the heart and tongue, and pen and hands too, as Paul's, day and night to work, rather than the progress and purity and simplicity of the crown of Christ Jesus should be debased or hindered.

This spirit will cause you to leave with joy, benefices, and bishopricks, worlds and lives for his sake; the heights and depths, lengths and breadths, of whose love you know doth infinitely pass your most knowing comprehensions and imaginations. There is but little of this spirit extant, I fear will not be, until we see Christ Jesus slain in the slaughter of the witnesses. Then Joseph will go boldly unto Pilate for the slaughtered body of most precious Saviour: and Nicodemus will go by day to buy and bestow his sweetest spices on his infinitely sweeter souls beloved. The full breathings of that heavenly spirit, unfeignedly and heartily wisheth you,

Your most unworthy countryman,

R. WILLIAMS."

26

No. V.—[p. 73.]

Rev. William Blackstone.

About the time that Roger Williams came to Providence, Rev. William Blackstone settled in Cumberland, near the river which bears his name, about three miles above Pawtucket. He was a man of learning, and had received Episcopal ordination in England. He appears to have left his native country, on account of his nonconformity, and he sought an asylum for the enjoyment of religious freedom in the wilds of New-England. The precise time of his arrival in this country is unknown. It appears from Johnson's History, p. 20, that he was here in 1628; but not agreeing with Mr. Endicot and others on ecclesiastical affairs, he devoted himself to agriculture. When the first planters of Massachusetts arrived, in the year 1630, they found him already quietly seated on the peninsula of *Shawmut*, now the city of Boston. His cottage was near a spring, on the south end of the peninsula. Gov. Hopkins, in his "History of Providence,"* says, that Mr. Blackstone had been at Boston "so long" (when Governor Winthrop and his company came) "as to have raised apple trees and planted an orchard." "Having escaped the power of the *Lords Bishops* in England, and

---

* His account of Providence was first published in the Providence Gazette, in 1765.

soon becoming discontented with the power of the
Lords Brethren here," he sold his lands on the peninsula, in the year 1635, and made a removal about
the year 1636. The place to which he removed,
was about six miles north of Mr. Williams. His
house was situated near the east bank of the river
which perpetuates his name, a few rods eastward
of a knoll, which he called "*Study Hill.*" It was
surrounded by a park, which was his favorite walk.
His house he named "*Study Hall.*" Here, also, he
planted an orchard, the first that ever bore apples
in Rhode-Island. "Many of the trees which he
planted, about one hundred and thirty years ago,"
says Governor Hopkins, in 1765, "are still pretty
thrifty fruit-bearing trees. He had the first of that
sort called yellow sweetings, that were ever in the
world, perhaps the richest and most delicious apple
of the whole kind." Mr. Blackstone used frequently to preach in Providence and other places
adjacent. He was a man of talent, and though
somewhat eccentric, sustained the character of an
exemplary Christian. He died, May 26, 1675,
having lived in New-England, about fifty years.
His death occurred at a critical period, a few
weeks before the commencement of *Philip's War.*
His estate was desolated, and his house and library
laid in ashes, by the ruthless natives. He lies
buried about two rods east of his favorite Study
Hill, where two rude stones designate the place of
his interment. His family here is extinct; but his

name will be found on the first list of freemen of Massachusetts, 1630, and it is identified with the beautiful stream which flows through the valley of the Blackstone.

No. VI.—[p. 74]

Deed of the chief Sachems of Narragansett to Roger Williams.

At Nanhiggansick, the 24th of the first month commonly called March, in the second year of our plantation, or planting at Mooshausick, or Providence : Memorandum, that we Caunannicus and Miantinomu, the two chief sachems of Nanhiggansick, having two years since sold unto Roger Williams the lands and meadows upon the two fresh rivers called Mooshausick and Wanaskatucket,* do now by these presents establish and confirm the bounds of those lands, from the rivers and fields of Pautuckett, the great hill of Neoterconkenitt† on the north-west, and the town of Mashapauge on the west. As also, in consideration of the many kindnesses and services he hath continually done for us, both for our friends of Massachusetts, as also at Quininkticutt and Apaum, or Plymouth ;

* The first of these rivers falls into the cove above Weybosset bridge from the north, the other from the west.

† Neoterconkernitt is three miles from Weybosset bridge, Mashapauge is about two miles south of Neoterconkenitt.

we do freely give unto him all that land from those rivers reaching to Pautuxett river, as also the grass and meadows upon Pautuxett river. In witness whereof we have hereunto set our hands.

The mark of 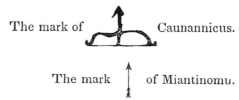 Caunannicus.

The mark of Miantinomu.

In presence of
The mark ⋈ of Seatagh.
The mark * of Assotemewett.

1639. Memorandum, 3d month, 9th day this was all again confirmed by Miantinomu. He acknowledged this his act and hand [illegible] up the stream of Pautuckett and Pautuxett without limits we might have for our use of cattle.

Witness hereof,
ROGER WILLIAMS,
BENEDICT ARNOLD.

[Providence Records.]

This deed is dated two years after the settlement of Mr. Williams and his associates at Providence, and bears date the same day and year, with the deed of Aquetneck or the Island of Rhode-Island. Previous to his banishment, he had cultivated an acquaintance with the natives, learned their language, and entered into negotiations for lands with the sachems Canonicus and Ousamequin, provided he should be under the necessity of settling among them. He had made large presents to these chiefs, "and therefore," says he, in one of his letters, " when I came, I was welcome to Ousamequin and to the old prince Canonicus, who was most shy of all English to his last breath."

No. VII.—[p. 74.]

Deed of Roger Williams to his twelve original associates.

PROVIDENCE, 8th of the 8th month, 1638,
(so called,)

Memorandum, that I, Roger Williams, having formerly purchased of Caunannicus and Miantinomu, this our situation, or plantation, of New-Providence, viz. the two fresh rivers, Wanasquatuckett and Mooshausick, and the ground and meadows thereupon; in consideration of thirty pounds received from the inhabitants of said place, do freely and fully pass, grant and make over equal right and power of enjoying and disposing of the same grounds and lands unto my loving friends and neighbors, Stukely Wescott, William Arnold, Thomas James, Robert Cole, John Greene, John Throckmorton, William Harris, William Carpenter, Thomas Olney, Francis Weston, Richard Waterman, Ezekiel Holliman, and such others as the major part of us shall admit into the same fellowship of vote with us :—As also I do freely make and pass over equal right and power of enjoying and disposing of the lands and grounds reaching from the aforesaid rivers unto the great river Pautuxett, with the grass and meadows thereupon, which was so lately given and granted by the aforesaid sachems to me.   Witness my hand,

ROGER WILLIAMS.

[Providence Records.]

Every inhabitant who was received, signed the following covenant :

" We whose names are here under-written, being desirous to inhabit in the town of Providence, do promise to submit ourselves, in active or passive obedience, to all such orders or agreements as shall be made for public good of the body, in an orderly way, by the major consent of the present inhabitants, masters of families, incorporated together into a township, and such others whom they shall admit unto the same, *only in civil things.*"

———

No. VIII.—[p. 74.]

Deposition of Roger Williams.

Narragansett, 18 June, 1682, Ut. Vul.

I testify as in the presence of the all making and all seeing God, that about fifty years since, I coming into this Narragansett country, I found a great contest between three sachems, two (to wit, Cononicus and Miantonomy)

were against Ousamaquin on Plymouth side, I was forced
to travel between them three, to pacify, to satisfy all their,
and their dependents' spirits of my honest intentions to
live peaceably by them.   I testify that it was the general
and constant declaration that Cononicus his father had
three sons, whereof Cononicus was the heir, and his
youngest brother's son Miantonomy (because of his youth)
was his Marshal and Executioner, and did nothing without his uncle Cononicus' consent.   And therefore I declare to posterity that were it not for the favor that God
gave me with Cononicus, none of these parts, no, not
Rhode-Island had been purchased or obtained, for I never
got any thing out of Cononicus but by gift.   I also profess
that being inquisitive of what root the title or denomination Nahiganset should come, I heard that Nahiganset
was so named from a little Island between Puttisquom-
scut and Musquomacuk on the sea and fresh water side.
I went on purpose to see it, and about the place called
Sugar-loaf Hill, I saw it, and was within a pole of it, but
could not learn why it was called Nahiganset.   I had
learnt that the Massachusetts was called so from the Blue
Hills, a little Island thereabout : and Cononicus' father and
ancestors living in those southern parts, transferred and
brought their authority and name into those northern parts
all along by the sea side, as appears by the great destruction of wood all along near the sea side : and I desire posterity to see the gracious hand of the Most High, (in
whose hands is all hearts,) that when the hearts of my
countrymen and friends and brethren failed me, his infinite wisdom and merits stirred up the barbarous heart of
Cononicus to love me as his son to his last gasp, by
which means I had not only Miantonomy and all the

Cowesit sachems my friends, but Ousamaquin also, who because of my great friendship with him at Plymouth and the authority of Cononicus, consented freely (being also well gratified by me) to the Governor Winthrop's and my enjoyment of Prudence, yea of Providence itself, and all the other lands I procured of Cononicus which were upon the point, and in effect whatsoever I desired of him. And I never denied him nor Miantonomy whatever they desired of me as to goods or gifts, or use of my boats or pinnace and the travels of my own person day and night, which though men know not nor care to know, yet the all-seeing eye hath seen it and his all-powerful hand hath helped me. Blessed be his holy name to eternity.

R. WILLIAMS.

September 28, 1704, I then being present at the house of Mr. Nathaniel Coddington, there, being presented with this written paper which I attest upon oath to be my father's own hand writing.

JOSEPH WILLIAMS, Assistant.

February 11, 1705. True copy of the orignal placed to record and examined by me.

WESTON CLARKE, Recorder.

[Colony Records.]

No. IX.—[p. 83.]

Biographical notice of Rev. John Clarke.

Dr. JOHN CLARKE, the founder and first Pastor of the first Baptist Church in Newport, was born October 8, 1609. He married Elizabeth, daughter of John Harges, Esq., of Bedfordshire, England. In a power of attorney he signed, May 12, 1656, to receive a legacy given by his wife's father out of the manor of Wreslingworth in Bedfordshire, he styles himself, John Clarke, Physician, of London. It is not certainly known where Mr. Clarke was born, but tradition makes him a native of Bedfordshire. His writings evince him to have been a learned man. In his will he bequeaths to his dear friend, Richard Bailey, his Hebrew and Greek books; also a Concordance and Lexicon, written by himself, the fruit of several years study. He published in London, in 1652, a book, entitled, "Ill News from New-England, or a narrative of New-England's persecution; wherein it is declared, that while Old England is becoming New, New-England is becoming Old, &c. &c.," in which he introduced the substance of a tract, issued the preceding year, called " A Brief Discourse touching New-England, and particularly Rhode-Island; as also a faithful and true relation of the prosecution of Obadiah Holmes, John Crandall and John Clarke, merely for conscience towards God, by the principal members of the Church or Commonwealth of the Massachusetts in New-England, which rules over that part of the world." This tract was probably written by the same hand.

In 1651, he was sent to England with Roger Williams to promote the interests of the Colony of Rhode-Island. Mr. Clarke remained in England, as agent for the Colony, till he procured the Charter of 1663. After his return, he was elected three years, successively, Deputy-Governor. But all his exertions to promote the civil prosperity of Rhode-Island, did not induce him to neglect the affairs of religion. He continued the esteemed pastor of the first Baptist Church in Newport, till his death. Having no children, he gave most of his property to charitable purposes; the income of which was to be given to the poor, and to be employed for the interests of learning and religion. He died, April 20, 1676, in the sixty-seventh year of his age, resigning his soul to his merciful Redeemer, and through faith in him he enjoyed the hope of a resurrection to eternal life. He left behind a writing which evinces his sentiments to have been those of the Particular Baptists. He was a faithful and useful minister, courteous and amiable in all the relations of life, and an ornament to his profession and to the several offices which he sustained. His memory is deserving of lasting honor for his efforts towards establishing the first government in the world,

which gave to all equal civil and religious liberty.
To no man, except Roger Williams, is Rhode-
Island more indebted than to him. He was the
original projector of the settlement on the Island,
and one of its ablest legislators. No character in
New-England is of purer fame than John Clarke.

> —————————————" all his study bent
> To worship God aright, and know his works
> Not hid, nor those things last which might preserve
> Freedom and Peace to men."—*Milton, P. L.* 11. 577.

From his three brothers, Thomas, Joseph and
Carew, are descended the large family in Rhode-
Island bearing the name of Clarke.

No. X.—[p. 84.]

The following is the form of civil compact agreed
to by the first settlers on the Island of Rhode-
Island.

"We whose names are underwritten do here solemnly,
in the presence of JEHOVAH, incorporate ourselves into a
body politic, and as he shall help, will submit our persons,
lives, and estates, unto our Lord Jesus Christ, the King
of kings and Lord of lords, and to all those perfect and

most absolute laws of his, given us in his holy word of truth to be guided and judged thereby."—*Exod.* 24. 3, 4. *II. Chron.* 11. 3.   *II. Kings*, 11. 17.

The first act passed under this form is dated 3d month 13th day, 1638, and is in these words.

" It is ordered that none shall be received as inhabitants or freemen, to build or plant upon the Island, but such as shall be received in by the consent of the body, and do submit to the government that is or shall be established according to the word of God."

This form continued till the 12th of March, 1640. On the 16th of March, 1641, at a General Court of Election,

" It was ordered and unanimously agreed upon, that the government which this body politic doth attend unto in this Island and the jurisdiction thereof, in favor of our Prince is a DEMOCRACY or popular government, (that is to say) it is in the power of the body of freemen, orderly assembled, or major part of them, to make or constitute just laws by which they will be regulated, and to depute from among themselves such ministers as shall see them faithfully executed between man and man.

" It was further ordered by the authority of this present Court, that no one be accounted a delinquent for DOCTRINE, provided it be not directly repugnant to the government or laws established."

And on the 17th September following (1641) they passed this act.

" It is ordered that that law of the last Court, made concerning liberty of conscience in point of doctrine, is perpetuated."

————

No. XI.—[p. 86.]

*Indian Deed of the Island of Aquetneck or Aquedneck.** *

The 24th of the 1st month called March in the year (so commonly called) 1637–8.

Memorandum, that we Cannonicus and Miantunnomu, the two chief sachems of the Nanhiggansets by virtue of our general command of this Bay ; as also the particular subjecting of the dead sachem of Aquedneck and Kitackamuckqut themselves and lands unto us, have sold unto Mr. Coddington and his friends united unto him, the great Island of Aquedneck, lying from hence eastward in this Bay, as also the marsh or grass upon Quinunnugat and the rest of the Islands in the Bay, (excepting Chibachuweca, formerly sold unto Mr. Winthrope, the now Governor of Massachusetts, and Mr. Williams of Providence) as also the rivers and coves about Kitackamuckqut and from

* This word is also spelled Aquethnick, Aquidneck, and Aquithneck ; the middle syllable was probably guttural.

thence to Paupasquash for the full payment of forty fathom of white beads to be equally divided between us. In witness whereof we have here subscribed.

Item. That by giving by Miantunnomu's hand ten coats and twenty hoes to the present inhabitants, they shall remove themselves from off the Island before next winter. Witness our hands.

The mark of 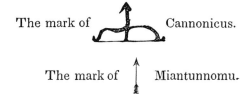 Cannonicus.

The mark of │ Miantunnomu.

In the presence of
The mark ⋈ of Yotursh,
ROGER WILLIAMS,
RANDAL HOLDEN,
The mark ⋈ of Assotimuit,
The mark ⋈ of Mishammoh,
      Cannonicus his son.

This witnesseth, that I, Wanamataunemet, the present sachem inhabitant of the Island, have received five fathom of wampum, and do consent to the contents.
      Witness my hand,

The mark of 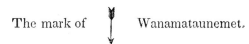 Wanamataunemet.

In the presence of
RANDAL HOLDEN.

Memorandum. That I Ousamequin, freely consent that Mr. William Coddington and his friends united unto him, shall make use of any grass or trees on the main land on Powakasick side, and do promise loving and just carriage of myself and all my men to the said Mr. Coddington, and English his friends united to him, having received of Mr. Coddington five fathom of wampum as gratuity from himself and the rest.

The mark ✕ of Ousamequin.

Dated the 6th day of the 5th month 1638.

Witness,
ROGER WILLIAMS,
RANDAL HOLDEN.

A true copy pr. me,

FRA. BRINLEY, Recorder.

A true copy pr. me,

WILLIAM LYTHERLAND, Recorder.

The 11th day of May, 1639. Received by me Miantunnomu (as a gratuity) of Mr. Coddington and his friends united, for my pains and travel in removing of the natives off the Island of Aquedneck, ten fathom of wampum peage and one broad cloth coat.

Mian ↑ tonnomu.

A true copy of the original entered and recorded by
JOHN SANFORD, Recorder.

Dated May 14th, 1639. Received of William Coddington and his friends united unto him, in full satisfaction for ground broken up or any other title or claim whatsoever formerly had of the Island of Aquedneck, the full sum of five fathom of wampum peage and a coat.

Weshaganasett ⋈ his mark.

Witness,

Miantonnomu his mark,

HUGH DURDAL,
Thomas Sabery ⋈ his mark.

A true copy of the original entered and recorded by me,

JOHN SANFORD, Recorder.

June 20th, 1639. Received of Mr. William Coddington and of his friends united to him in full satisfaction of ground broken up or any other title or claim whatsoever formerly had of the Island of Aquedneck, the full sum of five fathom of wampum peage.

Wonimenatony ⋈ his mark.

Witness,
WM. COWLING,
RICHARD SAWELL.

A true copy of the original entered and recorded by me,

JOHN SANFORD, Recorder.

The 22d November, 1639. Received by me Miantunnomu, of Mr. William Coddington and his friends

28

united, twenty and three coats and thirteen hoes to distribute to the Indians that did inhabit of the Island of Aquedneck, in full of all promises, debts and demands for the said Island, as also two tarkepes.

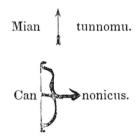

Mian   tunnomu.

Can   nonicus.

Witness,

AMOMPOUCKE,

WAMPAMINAQUITT.

A true copy of the original entered and recorded by
JOHN SANFORD, Recorder.

[Colony Records.]

The other seventeen joint purchasers of Aquetneck, whose names are mentioned p. 84, note, expressed their dissatisfaction that the Indian title to the Island of Rhode-Island stood in the name of Wm. Coddington, and to pacify them he executed an instrument of the following tenor, giving them an equal share with himself.

Boston in Massachusetts Bay in New-England.— Whereas, there was an agreement of eighteen persons to make purchase of some place to the southward for a plantation, whither they resolved to remove, for which end some of them were sent out to view a place for themselves and such others as they should take into the liberty of freemen and purchasers with them, and, upon their view was purchased Rhode-Island, with some small neighboring Islands and privileges of grass and wood of the Islands in the Bay and main adjoining ; and whereas, the sale of the said purchase from the Indians hath ever since lain in the hands of William Coddington, Esq., which being a great trouble to the aforesaid purchasers and freemen, I, the said William Coddington, Esq., do by this writing promise to deliver the said deeds of the purchase, together with what records are in my hands belonging to the said purchasers and freemen, into the hands of such as the major part of the purchasers and freemen shall appoint to receive them ; and do hereby declare that I, the said William Coddington, Esq., have no more in the purchase of right than any other of the purchasers or freemen received, or shall be received in by them, but only for my own proportion. In witness hereof, I have put to my hand this 14th of April, 1652.

WILLIAM CODDINGTON.

Signed in the presence of
ROBERT KNIGHT,
GEORGE MUNING.

A true copy of the original entered and recorded the 7th of April, 1673, by me,

JOHN SANFORD, Recorder.

[Colony Records.]

No. XII.—[p. 86.]

Deposition of William Coddington.

William Coddington, Esq., aged about seventy-six years old, testifyeth upon his engagement that when he was one of the magistrates of the Massachusetts Colony, he was one of the persons that made a peace with Cononicus and Miantonomy in the Colony's behalf with all the Narragansett Indians, and by order from the authority of the Massachusetts a little before they made war with the Pequod Indians. Not long after, this deponent went from Boston to find a plantation to settle upon, came to Aquedneck, now called Rhode-Island, where was a sachem called Wonnumetonomey, and this deponent went to buy the Island of him; but his answer was that Cononicus and Miantonomy were the chief sachems, and he could not sell the land, whereupon this deponent with some others went from Aquedneck Island into the Narragansett to the said sachems, Cononicus and Miantonomy, and bought the Island of them, they having as I understood the chief command both of the Narragansett and Aquedneck Island, and farther saith not. Taken upon engagement in Newport on Rhode-Island the 27th day of September 1677 before P. Sanford Assistant.

The above is a true copy of the original, placed to record, examined by me February 11, 1705.

WESTON CLARKE, Recorder.

[Colony Records.]

No. XIII.—[p. 89.]

For an able and an impartial account of Gorton and his religious opinions, the reader is referred to vol. 2 of the Collections of the Rhode-Island Historical Society, by the Hon. William R. Staples. We are gratified to learn that this gentleman is preparing for publication, a History of Providence.

[p. 92.]

For an early History of Narragansett, see vol. 3 of the Collections of the Rhode-Island Historical Society, by Elisha R. Potter, Esq. This work will supply valuable materials for the future historian of Rhode-Island.

No. XIV.—[p. 98.]

The first Patent of Rhode-Island.

Whereas, by an ordinance of the Lords and Commons now assembled in Parliament, bearing date the 2d day of November, Anno. Dom. 1643, Robert, Earl of Warwick, is constituted and ordained Governor in chief and Lord High Admiral of all those Islands and other Plantations, inhabited and planted by or belonging to any his Majesty the King of England's subjects, or which hereafter may be inhabited and planted by or belonging to them, within the bounds and upon the coast of America. And whereas, the said Lords and Commons have thought fit, and thereby ordained that Philip, Earl of Pembroke; Edward, Earl of Manchester; William, Viscount Say and Seal; Philip, Lord Wharton; John, Lord Roberts; Members of the House of Peers; Sir Gilbert Gerard, Baronet; Sir Arthur Haselrige, Baronet; Sir Henry Vane, Jr., Knight; Sir Benjamin Rudyerd, Knight; John Pym, Oliver Cromwell, Dennis Bond, Miles Corbet, Cornelius Holland, Samuel Vassall, John Rolle and William Spurstowe, Esq'rs, Members of the House of Commons, should be Commissioners, to join in aid and assistance with the said Earl.   And whereas, for the better governing and preserving of the said Plantations, it is thereby ordained, that the aforesaid Governor and Commissioners, or the greater number of them, should have power and authority from time to time, to nominate, appoint and constitute, all such subordinate governors, councils, commanders, officers and agents, as they should judge to be best affected, and most fit and serviceable to govern the said Islands and Plantations, and to provide for, order and dispose all things which they should from time to time find most fit and advantageous for the said Plantation, and for the better security of the owners and inhabitants thereof; to assign, ratify and confirm so much of their aforementioned authority and power, and in such manner and to such persons as they should judge to be fit for the better governing and preserving of the said Plantations and Islands from open violence, prejudice, disturbance and distractions.   And whereas there is a tract of land in the continent of America aforesaid, called by the name of the Narragansett Bay, bordering north and north-east on the

Robert
Warwick.

[L. S.]

Patent of Massachusetts, east and south-east on Plymouth Patent, south on the Ocean, and on the west and North-west, inhabited by Indians called Narrogunneucks, alias Narragansetts; the whole tract extending about twenty and five English miles unto the Pequot river and country. And whereas divers well affected and industrious English inhabitants of the towns of Providence, Portsmouth and Newport, in the tract aforesaid, have adventured to make a nearer neighborhood and society to and with that great body of the Narragansetts, which may in time, by the blessing of God upon their endeavors, lay a surer foundation of happiness to all America; and have also purchased, and are purchasing of and amongst the said natives, some other places, which may be convenient both for plantation, and also for the building of ships, supply of pipe-staves and other merchandize. And whereas, the said English have represented their desires to the said Earl and Commissioners, to have their hopeful beginning approved and confirmed by granting unto them a free charter of civil incorporation and government, that they may order and govern their Plantations in such manner as to maintain justice and peace, both amongst themselves and towards all men, with whom they shall have to do.

In due consideration of the premises, the said Robert, Earl of Warwick, Governor in chief and Lord High Admiral of the said Plantations, and the greater number of the said Commissioners, whose names and seals are here under written and subjoined, out of a desire to encourage the good beginnings of the said Plantations, do, by the authority of the aforesaid ordinance of Lords and Commons, give, grant and confirm unto the aforesaid inhabitants of the towns of Providence, Portsmouth and New-port, a free and absolute Charter of Civil Incorporation to be known by the name of *Incorporation of Providence Plantations, in the Narragansett Bay in New-England ;* together with full power and authority to govern and rule themselves and such others as shall hereafter inhabit with-in any part of the said tract of land, by such a form of civil government as by voluntary consent of all or the greatest part of them, shall be found most serviceable in their estates and condition ; and to that end, to make and ordain such civil laws and constitutions, and to inflict such punishments upon transgressors, and for execution thereof so to place and displace officers of justice, as they or the greatest part of them, shall by free consent agree unto.

Provided, nevertheless ; that the said laws, constitutions and punishments, for the civil government of the said plantation, be conformable to the laws of England, so far as the nature and constitution of that place will admit ; and always reserving to the said Earl and Commissioners, and their successors, power and authority so to dispose the General Government of that, as it stands in reference to the rest of the plantations in America, as they shall com-missionate from time to time, most conducing to the general good of the said Plantation, the honor of his Majesty, and the service of this State.

And the said Earl and Commissioners do further au-thorize the aforesaid inhabitants, and for the better transact-ing of their public affairs, to make and use a public seal, as the known seal of Providence Plantations, in the Nar-ragansett Bay in New-England.

In testimony whereof, the said Robert, Earl of Warwick, and Commissioners, have hereunto set their hands and seals, the seventeenth day of March, in the nineteenth year of the reign of our Sovereign Lord, King Charles, and in the year of our Lord God, 1643.

PEMBROKE,	[L. S.]
SAY AND SEAL,	[L. S.]
PHILIP WHARTON,	[L. S.]
ARTHUR HASELRIGE,	[L. S.]
COR. HOLLAND,	[L. S.]
H. VANE,	[L. S.]
SAM. VASSAL,	[L. S.]
JOHN ROLLE,	[L. S.]
MILES CORBET,	[L. S.]

RHODE-ISLAND, ss.

The aforegoing Charter or Patent is a true copy of the original entered and compared, April 10th, 1721.

Per   RICHARD WARD, Recorder.

[Colony Records.]

All the printed copies of the first Charter which the editor has seen, differ in several forms of expression, from the one on the Colony Records, in the office of the Secretary of State, from which the above copy is taken. This is one special reason for its publication here, although it has been introduced into the two preceding volumes of the Collections of the Rhode-Island Historical Society. The editor would here correct a slight error which has dropped from the pen of Mr. Savage, in his admirable edition of Winthrop, vol. 2, p. 193. He says, speaking of the first Charter, "Callender erroneously gives the date 17th of March." The reader will perceive, by a reference to the above copy, that Callender is correct. The copies generally have the date 14th of March.

No. XV.—[p. 98.]

Mr. Williams landed at Boston, September 17, 1644.* He brought with him the following letter from several noblemen and other members of the British Parliament, addressed "To the Right Worshipful the Governor and Assistants, and the rest of our worthy friends in the plantation of Massachusetts Bay, in New-England."

"Our much honored Friends:

Taking notice, some of us of long time, of Mr. Roger Williams his good affections and conscience, and of his sufferings by our common enemies and oppressors of God's people the prelates, as also of his great industry and travail in his printed Indian labors in your parts,† (the like where-

---

* See Savage's Winthrop, vol. 2, p. 193.

† His Key to the Indian language here alluded to, was published in London, 1643. The first volume of the Collections of the Rhode-Island Historical Society contains an edition of this work.

of we have not seen extant from any part of America,) and in which respect it hath pleased both Houses of Parliament to grant unto him, and friends with him, a free and absolute Charter of civil government for those parts of his abode ; and withal sorrowfully resenting, that amongst good men (our friends) driven to the ends of the world, exercised with the trials of a wilderness, and who mutually give good testimony, each of the other, (as we observe you do of him, and he abundantly of you,) there should be such a distance ; we thought it fit, upon divers considerations, to profess our great desires of both your utmost endeavors of nearer closing and of ready expressing those good affections, (which we perceive you bear to each other) in effectual performance of all friendly offices. The rather because of those bad neighbors you are likely to find in Virginia, and the unfriendly visits from the west of England and of Ireland : That howsoever it may please the Most High to shake our foundations, yet the report of your peaceable and prosperous plantations may be some refreshment to

Your true and faithful friends,

NORTHUMBERLAND,	P. WHARTON,
ROB. HARLEY,	THOS. BARRINGTON,
WM. MASHAM,	OL. ST. JOHN,
JOHN GURDON,	ISAAC PENNINGTON,
COR. HOLLAND,	GIL. PYKERING,
J. BLAKISTON,	MILES CORBET."

No. XVI.—[p. 98.]

Laws of Rhode-Island, 1647.

The first election under the Charter from the Earl of Warwick, &c., was held at Portsmouth, May 19th, 1647. The General Assembly then erected an institution of civil government, and established a code of laws, which is introduced with the following words.

"For the Province of Providence,

"Forasmuch as we have received from our Noble Lords and Honored Governors, and that by virtue of an Ordinance of the Parliament of England, a free and absolute Charter of civil incorporation, &c. We do jointly agree to incorporate ourselves, and so to remain a body politic by the authority thereof. And therefore do declare to own ourselves and one another to be members of the same body, and to have right to the freedom and privileges thereof, by subscribing our names to these words following, viz.

" We whose names are here underwritten, do engage ourselves, to the utmost of our estates and strength, to maintain the authority, and to enjoy the liberty granted to us by our Charter, in the extent of it according to the letter, and to maintain each other, by the same authority, in his lawful right and liberty.

And now sith our Charter gives us power to govern ourselves, and such other as come among us, and by such a form of civil government as by the voluntary consent, &c., shall be found most suitable to our estate and condition. It is agreeed by this present Assembly, thus incorporate, and by this present act declared, that the form of government established in Providence Plantations is DEMOCRATICAL,* that is to say, a government held by the free and voluntary consent of all, or the greater part of the free inhabitants.

" And now to the end that we may give each to other (notwithstanding our different consciences touching the truth as it is in Jesus, whereof upon the point we all make mention) as good and hopeful assurance as we are able, touching each man's peaceable and quiet enjoyment of his lawful right and liberty, we do agree unto, and by the authority abovesaid enact, establish and confirm these orders following."

Among others,

" That no person in this Colony shall be taken or imprisoned, or be disseised of his lands or liberties, or be exiled or any otherwise molested or destroyed, but by the lawful judgment of his peers, or by some known law, and according to the *letter of it*, ratified and confirmed by the major part of the General Assembly, lawfully met, and orderly managed."

This excellent code concludes with these memorable words.

" These are the laws that concern all men, and these

' This word is recorded in large capitals.

are the penalties for the transgressions thereof, which, by common consent, are ratified and established throughout the whole Colony. And otherwise than thus, what is herein forbidden, all men may walk as their consciences persuade them, every one in the name of his God. AND LET THE SAINTS OF THE MOST HIGH WALK IN THIS COLONY WITHOUT MOLESTATION, IN THE NAME OF JEHOVAH THEIR GOD, FOR EVER AND EVER."—*Colony Records.*

An eminet American historian* justly observes,

" The annals of Rhode-Island, if written in the spirit of philosophy, would exhibit the forms of society under a peculiar aspect. Had the territory of the State corresponded to the importance and singularity of the principles of its early existence, the world would have been filled with wonder at the phenomena of its early history."

No. XVII.—[p. 99.]

Letter from O. Cromwell to Rhode-Island, when Dr. John Clarke was agent of the Colony, in England.

To our trusty and well beloved the President, Assistants, and Inhabitants of Rhode-Island, together with the

* See Bancroft's History of the United States. vol. 1, p. 380; a work distinguished for research, skilful and luminous arrangement, and graphical description.

rest of the Providence Plantations, in the Narragansett bay in New-England.

GENTLEMEN,

Your agent here hath represented unto us, some particulars concerning your government, which you judge necessary to be settled by us here. But by reason of the other great and weighty affairs of this Commonwealth, we have been necessitated to defer the consideration of them to a further opportunity; for the mean time we were willing to let you know, that you are to proceed in your government according to the tenor of your Charter, formerly granted on that behalf; taking care of the peace and safety of those plantations, that neither through any intestine commotions, or foreign invasions, there do arise any detriment, or dishonor to this Commonwealth, or yourselves, as far as you, by your care and diligence, can prevent. And as for the things which are before us, they shall, as soon as the other occasions will permit, receive a just and fitting determination. And so we bid you farewell, and rest

Your very loving friend

OLIVER P.

29 March, 1655.   [Colony Records.]

No. XVIII.

From the General Assembly to the Commissioners of the United Colonies.

Honored Gentlemen,

There hath been presented to our view, by our honored

President, a letter bearing date September 25th last, subscribed by the Honored Gentlemen Commissioners of the United Colonies, concerning a company of people (lately arrived in these parts of the world) commonly known by the name of Quakers; who are generally conceived pernicious, either intentionally, or at leastwise in effect, even to the corrupting of good manners, and disturbing the common peace and societies of the places where they arise or resort unto, &c.

Now whereas freedom of different consciences, to be protected from inforcements, was the principal ground of our Charter, both with respect to our humble suit for it, as also to the true intent of the honorable and renowned Parliament of England in granting of the same unto us; which freedom we still prize as the greatest happiness that men can possess in this world; therefore we shall, for the preservation of our civil peace and order, the more seriously take notice that those people, and any other that are here, or shall come amongst us, be impartially required, and to our utmost constrained, to perform all duties requisite towards the maintaining the right of his Highness, and the government of that most renowed Commonwealth of England, in this Colony; which is most happily included under the same dominions, and we so graciously taken into protection thereof. And in case they the said people called Quakers which are here, or shall arise or come among us, do refuse to submit to the doing all duties aforesaid, as training, watching, and such other engagements as are upon members of civil societies, for the preservation of the same in justice and peace; then we determine, yea and we resolve (however) to take and

make use of the first opportunity to inform our agent residing in England, that he may humbly present the matter (as touching the considerations premised, concerning
the aforenamed people called Quakers) unto the supreme
authority of England, humbly craving their advice and
order, how to carry ourselves in any further respect towards those people (*) that therewithal there may be
no damage, or infringement of that chief principle in our
Charter, concerning freedom of consciences. And we
also are so much the more encouraged to make our addresses unto the Lord Protector his Highness and government aforesaid, for that we understand there are, or have
been, many of the aforesaid people suffered to live in
England, yea, even in the heart of the nation. And thus
with our truly thankful acknowledgments of the honorable care of the honored gentlemen Commissioners of the
United Colonies, for the peace and welfare of the whole
country, as is expressed in their most friendly letter, we
shall at present take leave and rest,

Yours most affectionately, desirous of your honor and
welfare.

JOHN SANFORD, Clerk of the Assembly.

PORTSMOUTH, March 13th, 1657–58.

From the General Assembly of the Colony of Providence
Plantations.

To the much honored John Endicot, Gov. of the Massachusetts. To be also imparted to the Hond. Coms. of
the United Colonies at their next meeting, These.

[Colony Records.]

* Obliterated.

No. XIX.—[p. 99.]

Letter of Commissioners to John Clarke.

Worthy Sir and trusty friend, Mr. Clarke.

We have found not only your ability and diligence, but also your love and care to be such concerning the welfare and prosperity of this Colony, since you have been intrusted with the more public affairs thereof, surpassing that no small benefit, which formerly we had of your presence here at home, that we in all straits and incumbrances are emboldened to repair to you, for your further and continued counsel, care and help, finding that your solid and Christian demeanor hath gotten no small interest in the hearts of our superiors, those noble and worthy senators with whom you have had to do on our behalf, as it hath constantly appeared in your addresses made unto them, which we have by good and comfortable proof found, having plentiful experience thereof.

The last year we have laden you with much employment, which we were then put upon by reason of some too refractory among ourselves, wherein we appealed unto you for your advice, for the more public manifestation of it with respect to our superiors. But our intelligence it seems fell short in that great loss of the ship, which is conceived here to be cast away. We have now a new occasion, given by an old spirit, with respect to the Colonies about us, who seem to be offended with us, because of a sort of people called by the name of Quakers, who are come amongst us, and have raised up divers who seem at present to be of their spirit, whereat the Colonies about us seem to be offended with us, being the said people have their liberty amongst us, as entertained into our houses, or into any of our assemblies. And for the present, we have found no just cause to charge them with the breach of the civil peace, only they are constantly going forth amongst them about us, and vex and trouble them in point of their religion and spiritual state, though they return with many a foul scar in their bodies for the same. And the offences our neighbors take against us, is because we take not some course against the said people, either to expel them from among us, or take such courses against them as themselves do, who are in fear lest their religion should be corrupted by them. Concerning which displeasure that they seem to take, it was expressed to us in a solemn letter, written by the Commissioners of the United Colonies at their sitting, as though they would bring us in to act according to their scantling, or else take some course to do us greater displeasure. A copy of which letter we have herewith sent unto you, wherein you may perceive how they express themselves. As also we have herewith sent our present answer unto them to give you what light we may in this matter. There is one clause in their letter which plainly implies a threat, though covertly expressed, as their manner is, which we gather to be this, that as themselves (as we conceive) have been much awed, in point of their continued subjection to the State of England, lest, in case they should decline, England might prohibit all trade with them, both in point of exportation and importation of any commodities, which were an host sufficiently prevalent to subdue New-England, as not being able to subsist; even so they seem secretly to threaten us, by cutting us off from all commerce and trade with them. and thereby to disable us of any comfortable subsistence, being that the concourse of shipping, and so of all kind of commodities, is universally conversant amongst themselves; as also knowing that ourselves are not in a capacity to send out shipping of ourselves, which is in great measure occasioned by their oppressing of us, as yourself well knows; as in many other respects, so in this for one, that we cannot have any thing from them for the supply of our necessities, but in effect they make the prices, both of our commodities and their own also, because we have not English coin, but only that which passeth among these barbarians, and such commodities as are raised by the labor of our hands, as corn, cattle, tobacco and the like, to make payment in, which they will have at their own rate, or else not deal with us, whereby (though they gain extraordinarily by us) yet for the safeguard of their religion may seem to neglect themselves in that respect, for what will not men do for their God.

Sir, this is our earnest and present request unto you in this matter, that as you may perceive in our answer to the United Colonies, that we fly, as to our refuge in all civil respects, to his Highness and honorable Council, as not being subject to any others in matters of our civil State, so may it please you to have an eye and ear open in case our adversaries should seek to undermine us in our privileges granted unto us, and to plead our case in such sort as we may not be compelled to exercise any civil power over men's consciences, so long as human orders, in point of civility, are not corrupted and violated, which our neighbors about us do frequently practice, whereof many of us have large experience, and do judge it to be no less than a point of absolute cruelty.

Sir, the humble respects and acknowledgments of this Court and Colony, with our continued and unwearied desires and wishes after the comfortable, honorable and prosperous proceedings of his highness and honorable Council, in all their so weighty affairs, departs not out of our hearts, night or day, which we could humbly wish (if it might not be too much boldness) were presented.

Sir, we have not been unmindful of your great care and kindness of those our worthy friends and gentlemen in that supply of powder and shot, and being a barrel of furs was returned in that ship, whereof Mr. Garrat had the command, wherein was betwixt twenty and thirty pounds worth of goods shipped, the Colony hath taken order for the recruiting of that loss, which we cannot possibly get in readiness to send by this ship, but our intent is, God willing, to send by the next opportunity. And so with our hearty love and respects to yourself, we take our leave.

  Subscribed,

   JOHN SANFORD, Clerk of the Assembly.

From a Court of Commissioners held in Warwick, this present November the 5th, 1658.

     [Colony Records.]

The persecution of the Quakers commenced in 1656, and continued till September, 1661, when an order was received from King Charles II. requiring that neither capital nor corporal punishment should be inflicted on the Quakers, but that offenders should be sent to England. For an account of these persecutions and of the acts passed against the Quakers, see Neal's History of New-England, vol. 1, 311. Hutchinson, vol. 1, 197. Hazard, vol. 1, 630–632. Bancroft, vol. 1, 451–458. See also the Quaker accounts, by Besse, Gould, and Sewell.

The letter of the Commissioners to John Clarke, and the preceding document, reflect great credit upon the early settlers of Rhode-Island, and show how far they were in advance of the other Colonies and of the age in which they lived. The principles of religious freedom, which they clearly and consistently maintained, are now the rule of action adopted by all Christian sects.

Many of the most respectable persons in the Colony embraced the sentiments of the Society of Friends, among whom was Governor Coddington, who died a member of that denomination. Their Yearly Meeting, until his death, in 1678, was held at his house. The first meeting house of the Friends was erected at Newport, in the year 1700. The Yearly Meeting for New-England was then established at that place where it has ever since been held.

No. XX.—[p. 99.]

Commission to John Clarke, when in England as Agent for Rhode-Island.

Whereas we the Colony of Providence Plantations, in New-England, having a free Charter of incorporation given and granted unto us, in the name of King and Parliament of England, &c., bearing date An. Dom. one thousand six hundred forty-three, by virtue of which Charter this Colony hath been distinguished from the other Colonies in New-England, and have ever since, and at this time, maintained government and order in the same Colony by administering judgment and justice, according to the rules in our said Charter prescribed : And further, whereas there have been sundry obstructions emerging, whereby this Colony have been put to trouble and charge for the preservation and keeping inviolate those privileges and immunities, to us granted in the foresaid free Charter, which said obstructions arise from the claims and encroachments of neighbors about us to and upon some parts of the tract of land, mentioned in our Charter to be within the bounds of this Colony.

These are therefore to declare and make manifest unto all that may have occasion to peruse and consider of these presents, that this present and principal Court of this Colony, sitting and transacting in the name of his most gracious and royal Majesty Charles the second by the grace of God the most mighty and potent King of England, Scotland, France and Ireland, and all the dominions and territories thereunto belonging, &c. Do by these presents make, ordain and constitute, desire, authorize and appoint, our trusty and well beloved friend, Mr. John Clarke, physician, one of the members of this Colony, late inhabitant of Rhode-Island, in the same Colony, and now residing in Westminster, our undoubted agent and attorney, to all intents and purposes, lawfully tending unto the preservation of all and singular the privileges, liberties, boundaries and immunities of this Colony, as according unto the true intent and meaning of all contained in our said Charter, against all unlawful usurpations, intrusions and claims, of any person or persons, on any pretences, or by any combination whatsoever, not doubting but the same gracious hand of Providence, which moved the most potent and royal power abovesaid to give and grant us the abovesaid free Charter, will also still continue to preserve us, in our just rights and privileges, by the gracious favor of the power and royal Majesty abovesaid, whereunto we acknowledge all humble submission and loyal subjection, &c.

Given in the twelfth year of the reign of our Sovereign Lord, Charles the second, King of England, Scotland, France and Ireland, &c., at the General Court holden for the colony of Providence Plantations, at Warwick, the 18th day of October An: Dom. 1660.

To our trusty and well beloved friend and agent, Mr. John Clarke of Rhode-Island, Physician, now residing in London or Westminster.

Ordered to be subscribed by the General Recorder, with the seal of the Colony annexed.

[Colony Records.]

No. XXI.—[p. 100.]

The Charter granted by King Charles II., July 8, 1663.

CHARLES THE SECOND, by the grace of God, King of England, Scotland, France and Ireland, Defender of the Faith, &c., to all to whom these presents shall come, greeting : Whereas, we have been informed, by the humble petition of our trusty and well beloved subject, John Clarke, on the behalf of Benjamin Arnold, William Brenton, William Coddington, Nicholas Easton, William Boulston, John Porter, John Smith, Samuel Gorton, John Weeks, Roger Williams, Thomas Olney, Gregory Dexter, John Coggeshall, Joseph Clarke, Randall Holden, John Greene, John Roome, Samuel Wildbore, William Field, James Barker, Richard Tew, Thomas Harris, and William Dyre, and the rest of the purchasers and free inhabitants of our Island called Rhode-Island, and the rest of the Colony of Providence Plantations, in the Narragansett Bay, in New-England, in America, that they, pursuing, with peaceable and loyal minds, their sober, serious and religious intentions, of godly edifying themselves, and one another, in the holy Christian faith and worship, as they were persuaded ; together with the gaining over and conversion of the poor ignorant Indian natives, in those parts of America, to the sincere profession and obedience of the same faith and worship, did, not only by the consent and good encouragement of our royal progenitors, transport themselves out of this kingdom of England into America ; but also, since their arrival there, after their first settlement amongst other our subjects in those parts, for the avoiding of discord, and those many evils which were likely to ensue upon some of those our subjects not being able to bear, in these remote parts, their different apprehensions in religious concernments, and in pursuance of the aforesaid ends, did once again leave their desirable stations and habitations, and with excessive labor and travel, hazard and charge, did transplant themselves into the midst of the Indian natives, who, as we are informed, are the most potent princes and people of all that country; where, by the good Providence of God, from whom the Plantations have taken their name, upon their labor and industry, they have not only been preserved to admiration, but have increased and prospered, and are seized and possessed, by purchase and consent of the said natives, to their full content, of such lands, islands, rivers, harbors and roads, as are very convenient, both for plantations, and also for building of ships, supply of pipe-staves, and other merchandise ; and which lie very commodious, in many respects, for commerce, and to accommodate our southern plantations, and may much advance the trade of this our realm, and greatly enlarge the territories thereof; they having, by near neighborhood to, and friendly society with, the great body of the Narragansett Indians, given them encouragement, of their own accord, to subject themselves, their people and lands, unto us; whereby, as is hoped, there may, in time, by the blessing of God upon their endeavors, be laid a sure foundation of happiness to all America: And whereas, in their humble address, they have freely declared, that it is much on their hearts (if they may be permitted) to hold forth a lively experiment, that a most flourishing civil state may stand and best be maintained, and that among our English subjects, with a

full liberty in religious concernments ; and that true piety,
rightly grounded upon gospel principles, will give the
best and greatest security to sovereignty, and will lay in
the hearts of men the strongest obligations to true loyalty:
Now know ye, that we, being willing to encourage the
hopeful undertaking of our said loyal and loving subjects,
and to secure them in the free exercise and enjoyment of
all their civil and religious rights, appertaining to them,
as our loving subjects; and to preserve unto them that
liberty, in the true Christian faith and worship of God,
which they have sought with so much travel, and with
peaceable minds, and loyal subjection to our royal progenitors and ourselves, to enjoy ; and because some of
the people and inhabitants of the same Colony cannot, in
their private opinions, conform to the public exercise of
religion, according to the liturgy, forms and ceremonies
of the Church of England, or take or subscribe the oaths
and articles made and established in that behalf ; and for
that the same, by reason of the remote distances of those
places, will (as we hope) be no breach of the unity and
uniformity established in this nation : Have therefore
thought fit, and do hereby publish, grant, ordain and declare, That our royal will and pleasure is, that no person
within the said Colony, at any time hereafter, shall be any
wise molested, punished, disquieted, or called in question,
for any differences in opinion in matters of religion, and
do not actually disturb the civil peace of our said Colony ;
but that all and every person and persons may, from time
to time, and at all times hereafter, freely and fully have
and enjoy his and their own judgments and consciences,
in matters of religious concernments, throughout the tract
of land hereafter mentioned, they behaving themselves

peaceably and quietly, and not using this liberty to licentiousness and profaneness, nor to the civil injury or outward disturbance of others; any law, statute, or clause therein contained, or to be contained, usage or custom of this realm, to the contrary hereof, in any wise, notwithstanding. And that they may be in the better capacity to defend themselves, in their just rights and liberties, against all the enemies of the Christian faith, and others, in all respects, we have further thought fit, and at the humble petition of the persons aforesaid are graciously pleased to declare, That they shall have and enjoy the benefit of our late act of indemnity and free pardon, as the rest of our subjects in other our dominions and territories have; and to create and make them a body politic or corporate, with the powers and privileges hereinafter mentioned. And accordingly our will and pleasure is, and of our especial grace, certain knowledge, and mere motion, we have ordained, constituted and declared, and by these presents, for us, our heirs and successors, do ordain, constitute and declare, That they, the said William Brenton, William Coddington, Nicholas Easton, Benedict Arnold, William Boulston, John Porter, Samuel Gorton, John Smith, John Weeks, Roger Williams, Thomas Olney, Gregory Dexter, John Coggeshall, Joseph Clarke, Randall Holden, John Greene, John Roome, William Dyre, Samuel Wildbore, Richard Tew, William Field, Thomas Harris, James Barker, ———— Rainsborrow, ———— Williams, and John Nickson, and all such others as now are, or hereafter shall be, admitted and made free of the company and society of our Colony of Providence Plantations, in the Narragansett Bay, in New-England, shall be, from time to time, and forever hereafter, a body corporate and politic, in fact and name, by the name of *The Governor and Company of the English Colony of Rhode-Island and Providence Plantations, in New-England, in America;* and that, by the same name, they and their successors shall and may have perpetual succession, and shall and may be persons able and capable, in the law, to sue and be sued, to plead and be impleaded, to answer and be answered unto, to defend and to be defended, in all and singular suits, causes, quarrels, matters, actions and things, of what kind or nature soever; and also to have, take, possess, acquire and purchase, lands, tenements or hereditaments, or any goods or chattels, and the same to lease, grant, demise, aliene, bargain, sell and dispose of, at their own will and pleasure, as other our liege people, of this our realm of England, or any corporation or body politic within the same, may lawfully do. And further, that they the said Governor and Company, and their successors, shall and may, forever hereafter, have a common seal, to serve and use for all matters, causes, things and affairs, whatsoever, of them and their successors; and the same seal to alter, change, break, and make new, from time to time, at their will and pleasure, as they shall think fit. And further, we will and ordain, and by these presents, for us, our heirs and successors, do declare and appoint, that, for the better ordering and managing of the affairs and business of the said Company, and their successors, there shall be one Governor, one Deputy-Governor, and ten Assistants, to be, from time to time, constituted, elected and chosen, out of the freemen of the said Company, for the time being, in such manner and form as is hereafter in these presents expressed; which said officers shall apply themselves to take care for the best disposing and ordering of the general business and affairs of and concerning the lands and hereditaments hereinafter mentioned to be granted, and the plantation thereof, and the government of the people there. And, for the better execution of our royal pleasure herein, we do, for us, our heirs and successors, assign, name, constitute and appoint the aforesaid Benedict Arnold to be the first and present Governor of the said Company, and the said William Brenton to be the Deputy-Governor, and the said William Boulston, John Porter, Roger Williams, Thomas Olney, John Smith, John Greene, John Coggeshall, James Barker, William Field, and Joseph Clarke, to be the ten present Assistants of the said Company, to continue in the said several offices, respectively, until the first Wednesday which shall be in the month of May now next coming. And further, we will, and by these presents, for us, our heirs and successors, do ordain and grant, that the Governor of the said Company, for the time being, or, in his absence, by occasion of sickness, or otherwise, by his leave and permission, the Deputy-Governor, for the time being, shall and may, from time to time, upon all occasions, give order for the assembling of the said Company, and calling them together, to consult and advise of the business and affairs of the said Company. And that forever hereafter, twice in every year, that is to say, on every first Wednesday in the month of May, and on every last Wednesday in October, or oftener, in case it shall be requisite, the Assistants, and such of the freemen of the said Company, not exceeding six persons for Newport, four persons for each of the respective towns of Providence, Portsmouth and Warwick, and two persons for each other place, town or city, who shall be, from time to time, thereunto elected or deputed by the major part of the freemen of the respective towns or places for which they shall be so elected or deputed, shall have a general meeting or assembly, then and there to consult, advise and determine, in and about the affairs and business of the said Company and Plantations. And further, we do, of our especial grace, certain knowledge, and mere motion, give and grant unto the said Governor and Company of the English Colony of Rhode-Island and Providence Plantations, in New-England, in America, and their successors, that the Governor, or, in his absence, or by his permission, the Deputy-Governor of the said Company, for the time being, the Assistants, and such of the freemen of the said Company as shall be so as aforesaid elected or deputed, or so many of them as shall be present at such meeting or assembly, as aforesaid, shall be called the General Assembly; and that they, or the greatest part of them then present, whereof the Governor or Deputy-Governor, and six of the Assistants, at least to be seven, shall have, and have hereby given and granted unto them, full power and authority, from time to time, and at all times hereafter, to appoint, alter and change, such days, times and places of meeting and General Assembly, as they shall think fit; and to choose, nominate and appoint, such and so many other persons as they shall think fit, and shall be willing to accept the same, to be free of the said Company and body politic, and them into the same to admit; and to elect and constitute such offices and officers, and to grant such needful commissions, as they shall think fit and requisite, for the ordering, managing and despatching of the affairs of the said Governor and Company, and their successors; and, from time to time, to make, ordain,

constitute or repeal, such laws, statutes, orders and ordinances, forms and ceremonies of government and magis-
tracy, as to them shall seem meet, for the good and welfare of the said Company, and for the government and
ordering of the lands and hereditaments, hereinafter mentioned to be granted, and of the people that do, or at any
time hereafter shall, inhabit or be within the same ; so as
such laws, ordinances and constitutions, so made, be not
contrary and repugnant unto, but, as near as may be,
agreeable to the laws of this our realm of England, considering the nature and constitution of the place and people there ; and also to appoint, order and direct, erect and
settle, such places and courts of jurisdiction, for the hear-
ing and determining of all actions, cases, matters and
things, happening within the said Colony and Plantation,
and which shall be in dispute, and depending there, as
they shall think fit; and also to distinguish and set forth
the several names and titles, duties, powers and limits, of
each court, office and officer, superior and inferior ; and
also to contrive and appoint such forms of oaths and at-
testations, not repugnant, but, as near as may be, agreeable,
as aforesaid, to the laws and statutes of this our realm, as
are convenient and requisite, with respect to the due administration of justice, and due execution and discharge
of all offices and places of trust by the persons that shall
be therein concerned ; and also to regulate and order the
way and manner of all elections to offices and places of
trust, and to prescribe, limit and distinguish the numbers
and bounds of all places, towns or cities, within the limits
and bounds hereinafter mentioned, and not herein particularly named, who have, or shall have, the power of
electing and sending of freemen to the said General As-

sembly ; and also to order, direct and authorize the imposing of lawful and reasonable fines, mulcts, imprisonments, and executing other punishments, pecuniary and corporal, upon offenders and delinquents, according to the course of other corporations within this our kingdom of England ; and again to alter, revoke, annul or pardon, under their common seal, or otherwise, such fines, mulcts, imprisonments, sentences, judgments and condemnations, as shall be thought fit ; and to direct, rule, order and dispose of, all other matters and things, and particularly that which relates to the making of purchases of the native Indians, as to them shall seem meet ; whereby our said people and inhabitants, in the said Plantations, may be so religiously, peaceably and civilly governed, as that, by their good life and orderly conversation, they may win and invite the native Indians of the country to the knowledge and obedience of the only true God, and Saviour of mankind ; willing, commanding and requiring, and by these presents, for us, our heirs and successors, ordaining and appointing, that all such laws, statutes, orders and ordinances, instructions, impositions and directions, as shall be so made by the Governor, Deputy-Governor, Assistants and freemen, or such number of them as aforesaid, and published in writing, under their common seal, shall be carefully and duly observed, kept, performed and put in execution, according to the true intent and meaning of the same. And these our letters patent, or the duplicate or exemplification thereof, shall be to all and every such officers, superior and inferior, from time to time, for the putting of the same orders, laws, statutes, ordinances, instructions and directions, in due execution, against us, our heirs and successors, a sufficient warrant and discharge. And further, our will and pleasure is, and we do hereby, for us, our heirs and successors, establish and ordain, that yearly, once in the year, forever hereafter, namely, the aforesaid Wednesday in May, and at the town of Newport, or elsewhere, if urgent occasion do require, the Governor, Deputy-Governor and Assistants of the said Company, and other officers of the said Company, or such of them as the General Assembly shall think fit, shall be, in the said General Court or Assembly to be held from that day or time, newly chosen for the year ensuing, by such greater part of the said Company, for the time being, as shall be then and there present; and if it shall happen that the present Governor, Deputy-Governor and Assistants, by these presents appointed, or any such as shall hereafter be newly chosen into their rooms, or any of them, or any other the officers of the said Company, shall die or be removed from his or their several offices or places, before the said general day of election, (whom we do hereby declare, for any misdemeanor or default, to be removable by the Governor, Assistants and Company, or such greater part of them, in any of the said public courts, to be assembled as aforesaid,) that then, and in every such case, it shall and may be lawful to and for the said Governor, Deputy-Governor, Assistants and Company aforesaid, or such greater part of them, so to be assembled as is aforesaid, in any their assemblies, to proceed to a new election of one or more of their Company, in the room or place, rooms or places, of such officer or officers, so dying or removed, according to their discretions; and immediately upon and after such election or elections made of such Governor, Deputy-Governor, Assistant or Assistants, or any other officer of the said Company, in manner and form aforesaid, the authority, office and power, before given to the former Governor, Deputy-Governor, and other officer and officers, so removed, in whose stead and place new shall be chosen, shall, as to him and them, and every of them, respectively, cease and determine : *Provided always*, and our will and pleasure is, that as well such as are by these presents appointed to be the present Governor, Deputy-Governor and Assistants, of the said Company, as those that shall succeed them, and all other officers to be appointed and chosen as aforesaid, shall, before the undertaking the execution of the said offices and places respectively, give their solemn engagement, by oath, or otherwise, for the due and faithful performance of their duties in their several offices and places, before such person or persons as are by these presents hereafter appointed to take and receive the same, that is to say : the said Benedict Arnold, who is hereinbefore nominated and appointed the present Governor of the said Company, shall give the aforesaid engagement before William Brenton, or any two of the said Assistants of the said Company ; unto whom we do by these presents give full power and authority to require and receive the same ; and the said William Brenton, who is hereby before nominated and appointed the present Deputy-Governor of the said Company, shall give the aforesaid engagement before the said Benedict Arnold, or any two of the Assistants of the said Company ; unto whom we do by these presents give full power and authority to require and receive the same ; and the said William Boulston, John Porter, Roger Williams, Thomas Olney, John Smith, John Greene, John Coggeshall, James Barker, William Field, and Joseph Clarke, who are hereinbefore nominated and appointed the present Assistants of the said Company, shall give the said engagement to their officers and places respectively belonging, before the said Benedict Arnold and William Brenton, or one of them; to whom respectively we do hereby give full power and authority to require, administer or receive the same: and further, our will and pleasure is, that all and every other future Governor or Deputy-Governor, to be elected and chosen by virtue of these presents, shall give the said engagement before two or more of the said Assistants of the said Company for the time being; unto whom we do by these presents give full power and authority to require, administer or receive the same; and the said Assistants, and every of them, and all and every other officer or officers to be hereafter elected and chosen by virtue of these presents, from time to time, shall give the like engagements, to their offices and places respectively belonging, before the Governor or Deputy-Governor for the time being; unto which said Governor, or Deputy-Governor, we do by these presents give full power and authority to require, administer or receive the same accordingly. And we do likewise, for us, our heirs and successors, give and grant unto the said Governor and Company, and their successors, by these presents, that, for the more peaceable and orderly government of the said Plantations, it shall and may be lawful for the Governor, Deputy-Governor, Assistants, and all other officers and ministers of the said Company, in the administration of justice, and exercise of government, in the said Plantations, to use, exercise, and put in execution, such methods, rules, orders and directions, not being contrary or repugnant to the laws and statutes of this our realm, as have been heretofore given, used and accustomed, in such cases respectively, to be put in practice, until at the next, or some other General Assembly, special provision shall be made and ordained in the cases aforesaid. And we do further, for us, our heirs and successors, give and grant unto the said Governor and Company, and their successors, by these presents, that it shall and may be lawful to and for the said Governor, or in his absence, the Deputy-Governor, and major part of the said Assistants, for the time being, at any time when the said General Assembly is not sitting, to nominate, appoint and constitute, such and so many commanders, governors and military officers, as to them shall seem requisite, for the leading, conducting and training up the inhabitants of the said Plantations in martial affairs, and for the defence and safeguard of the said Plantations; and that it shall and may be lawful to and for all and every such commander, governor and military officer, that shall be so as aforesaid, or by the Governor, or, in his absence, the Deputy-Governor, and six of the said Assistants, and major part of the freemen of the said Company present at any General Assemblies, nominated, appointed and constituted, according to the tenor of his and their respective commissions and directions, to assemble, exercise in arms, martial array, and put in warlike posture, the inhabitants of the said Colony, for their special defence and safety ; and to lead and conduct the said inhabitants, and to encounter, expulse, expel and resist, by force of arms, as well by sea as by land, and also to kill, slay and destroy, by all fitting ways, enterprises and means whatsoever, all and every such person or persons as shall, at any time hereafter, attempt or enterprise the destruction, invasion, detriment or annoyance of the said inhabitants or Plantations ; and to use and exercise the law martial in such cases only as occasion shall necessarily require ; and to take or surprise, by all ways and means whatsoever, all and every such person and persons, with their ship or ships, armor, ammunition, or other goods of such persons as shall, in hostile manner, invade or attempt the defeating of the said Plantation, or the hurt of the said Company and inhabitants ; and, upon just causes, to invade and destroy the native Indians, or other enemies of the said Colony.   Nevertheless, our will and pleasure is, and we do hereby declare to the rest of our Colonies in New-England, that it shall not be lawful for this our Colony of Rhode-Island and Providence Plantations, in America, in New-England, to invade the natives inhabiting within the bounds and limits of their said Colonies, without the knowledge and consent of the said other Colonies.   And it is hereby declared, that it shall not be lawful to or for the rest of the Colonies to invade or molest the native Indians, or any other inhabitants, inhabiting within the bounds and limits hereafter mentioned, (they having subjected themselves unto us, and being by us taken into our special protection,) without the knowledge and consent of the Governor and Company of our Colony of Rhode-Island and Providence Plantations.   Also our will and pleasure is, and we do hereby declare unto all Christian Kings, Princes and States, that if any person, which shall hereafter be of the said Company or Plantation, or any other, by appointment of the said Governor and Company for the time being, shall, at any time or times hereafter, rob or spoil, by sea or land, or do any hurt or unlawful hostility to any of the subjects of us, our heirs or successors, or any of the subjects of any Prince or State, being

then in league with us, our heirs or successors, upon complaint of such injury done to any such Prince or State, or
their subjects, we, our heirs and successors, will make
open proclamation within any parts of our realm of England, fit for that purpose, that the person or persons com-
mitting any such robbery or spoil shall, within the time
limited by such proclamation, make full restitution or
satisfaction of all such injuries, done or committed, so as
the said Prince, or others so complaining, may be fully
satisfied and contented ; and, if the said person or persons
who shall commit any such robbery or spoil, shall not
make satisfaction, accordingly, within such time, so to be
limited, that then we, our heirs and successors, will put
such person or persons out of our allegiance and protection;
and that then it shall and may be lawful and free for all
Princes or others, to prosecute, with hostility, such offenders, and every of them, their and every of their pro-
curers, aiders, abettors and counsellors, in that behalf :
Provided also, and our express will and pleasure is, and
we do, by these presents, for us, our heirs and successors,
ordain and appoint, that these presents shall not, in any
manner, hinder any of our loving subjects, whatsoever,
from using and exercising the trade of fishing upon the
coast of New-England, in America ; but that they, and
every or any of them, shall have full and free power and
liberty to continue and use the trade of fishing upon the
said coast, in any of the seas thereunto adjoining, or any
arms of the seas, or salt water, rivers and creeks, where
they have been accustomed to fish ; and to build and set
upon the waste land, belonging to the said Colony and
Plantations, such wharves, stages and work-houses, as
shall be necessary for the salting, drying and keeping of

their fish, to be taken or gotten upon that coast. And further, for the encouragement of the inhabitants of our said Colony of Providence Plantations to set upon the business of taking whales, it shall be lawful for them, or any of them, having struck whale, dubertus, or other great fish, it or them to pursue unto any part of that coast, and into any bay, river, cove, creek or shore, belonging thereto, and it or them, upon the said coast, or in the said bay, river, cove, creek or shore, belonging thereto, to kill and order for the best advantage, without molestation, they making no wilful waste or spoil; any thing in these presents contained, or any other matter or thing, to the contrary notwithstanding. And further also, we are graciously pleased, and do hereby declare, that if any of the inhabitants of our said Colony do set upon the planting of vineyards (the soil and climate both seeming naturally to concur to the production of wines) or be industrious in the discovery of fishing banks, in or about the said Colony, we will, from time to time, give and allow all due and fitting encouragement therein, as to others in cases of like nature. And further, of our more ample grace, certain knowledge, and mere motion, we have given and granted, and by these presents, for us, our heirs and successors, do give and grant unto the said Governor and Company of the English Colony of Rhode-Island and Providence Plantations, in the Narragansett Bay, in New-England, in America, and to every inhabitant there, and to every person and persons trading thither, and to every such person or persons as are or shall be free of the said Colony, full power and authority, from time to time, and at all times hereafter, to take, ship, transport and carry away, out of any of our realms and dominions, for and towards the plantation and defence of the said Colony, such and so many of our loving subjects and strangers as shall or will willingly accompany them in and to their said Colony and Plantation ; except such person or persons as are or shall be therein restrained by us, our heirs and successors, or any law or statute of this realm : and also to ship and transport all and all manner of goods, chattels, merchandises, and other things whatsoever, that are or shall be useful or necessary for the said Plantations, and defence thereof, and usually transported, and not prohibited by any law or statute of this our realm ; yielding and paying unto us, our heirs and successors, such the duties, customs and subsidies, as are or ought to be paid or payable for the same. And further, our will and pleasure is, and we do, for us, our heirs and successors, ordain, declare and grant, unto the said Governor and Company, and their successors, that all and every the subjects of us, our heirs and successors, which are already planted and settled within our said Colony of Providence Plantations, or which shall hereafter go to inhabit within the said Colony, and all and every of their children, which have been born there, or which shall happen hereafter to be born there, or on the sea, going thither, or returning from thence, shall have and enjoy all liberties and immunities of free and natural subjects within any the dominions of us, our heirs or successors, to all intents, constructions and purposes, whatsoever, as if they, and every of them, were born within the realm of England. And further, know ye, that we, of our more abundant grace, certain knowledge and mere motion, have given, granted and confirmed, and, by these presents, for us, our heirs and successors, do give, grant and confirm, unto the said Governor and

Company, and their successors, all that part of our dominions in New-England, in America, containing the Na-
hantick and Nanhyganset, alias Narragansett Bay, and
countries and parts adjacent, bounded on the west, or
westerly, to the middle or channel of a river there, commonly called and known by the name of Pawcatuck, alias
Pawcawtuck river, and so along the said river, as the
greater or middle stream thereof reacheth or lies up into
the north country, northward, unto the head thereof, and
from thence, by a strait line drawn due north, until it
meets with the south line of the Massachusetts Colony ;
and on the north; or northerly, by the aforesaid south or
southerly line of the Massachusetts Colony or Plantation,
and extending towards the east, or eastwardly, three English miles to the east and north-east of the most eastern
and north-eastern parts of the aforesaid Narragansett Bay,
as the said bay lyeth or extendeth itself from the ocean
on the south, or southwardly, unto the mouth of the river
which runneth towards the town of Providence, and from
thence along the eastwardly side or bank of the said river
(higher called by the name of Seacunck river) up to the
falls called Patuckett falls, being the most westwardly
line of Plymouth Colony, and so from the said falls, in a
strait line, due north, until it meet with the aforesaid line
of the Massachusetts Colony ; and bounded on the south
by the ocean : and, in particular, the lands belonging to
the towns of Providence, Pawtuxet, Warwick, Misquam-
macock, alias Pawcatuck, and the rest upon the main land
in the tract aforesaid, together with Rhode-Island, Block-
Island, and all the rest of the islands and banks in the Narragansett Bay, and bordering upon the coast of the tract
aforesaid, (Fisher's Island only excepted,) together with

all firm lands, soils, grounds, havens, ports, rivers, waters, fishings, mines royal, and all other mines, minerals, precious stones, quarries, woods, wood-grounds, rocks, slates, and all and singular other commodities, jurisdictions, royalties, privileges, franchises, preheminences and hereditaments, whatsoever, within the said tract, bounds, lands and islands, aforesaid, or to them or any of them belonging, or in any wise appertaining : *to have and to hold* the same, unto the said Governor and Company, and their successors, forever, upon trust, for the use and benefit of themselves and their associates, freemen of the said Colony, their heirs and assigns, to be holden of us, our heirs and successors, as of the Manor of East-Greenwich, in our county of Kent, in free and common soccage, and not in capite, nor by knight service ; yielding and paying therefor, to us, our heirs and successors, only the fifth part of all the ore of gold and silver, which, from time to time, and at all times hereafter, shall be there gotten, had, or obtained, in lieu and satisfaction of all services, duties, fines, forfeitures, made or to be made, claims and demands whatsoever, to be to us, our heirs or successors, therefor or thereout rendered, made, or paid, any grant, or clause in a late grant, to the Governor and Company of Connecticut Colony, in America, to the contrary thereof in any wise notwithstanding ; the aforesaid Pawcatuck river having been yielded, after much debate, for the fixed and certain bounds between these our said Colonies, by the agents thereof ; who have also agreed, that the said Pawcatuck river shall be also called alias Norrogansett or Narrogansett river ; and, to prevent future disputes, that otherwise might arise thereby, forever hereafter shall be construed, deemed and taken to be the Narrogansett river

in our late grant to Connecticut Colony mentioned as the
easterly bounds of that Colony. And further, our will
and pleasure is, that in all matters of public controversy,
which may fall out between our Colony of Providence
Plantations, and the rest of our Colonies in New-England,
it shall and may be lawful to and for the Governor and
Company of the said Colony of Providence Plantations, to
make their appeals therein to us, our heirs and successors,
for redress in such cases, within this our realm of England : and that it shall be lawful to and for the inhabitants of the said Colony of Providence Plantations, without let or molestation, to pass and repass, with freedom,
into and through the rest of the English Colonies, upon
their lawful and civil occasions, and to converse, and hold
commerce and trade, with such of the inhabitants of our
other English Colonies as shall be willing to admit them
thereunto, they behaving themselves peaceably among
them ; any act, clause, or sentence, in any of the said
Colonies provided, or that shall be provided, to the contrary in any wise notwithstanding. And lastly, we do,
for us, our heirs and successors, ordain and grant unto the
said Governor and Company, and their successors, by
these presents, that these our letters patent shall be firm,
good, effectual, and available in all things in the law, to all
intents, constructions and purposes whatsoever, according
to our true intent and meaning hereinbefore declared ; and
shall be construed, reputed and adjudged in all cases most
favorably on the behalf, and for the best benefit and be-
hoof, of the said Governor and Company, and their successors ; although express mention of the true yearly
value or certainty of the premises, or any of them, or of
any other gifts or grants by us, or by any of our progeni-

tors or predecessors, heretofore made to the said Governor and Company of the English Colony of Rhode-Island and Providence Plantations, in the Narragansett Bay, New-England, in America, in these presents is not made, or any statute, act, ordinance, provision, proclamation or restriction, heretofore had, made, enacted, ordained or provided, or any other matter, cause or thing whatsoever, to the contrary thereof in any wise notwithstanding. In witness whereof, we have caused these our letters to be made patent. Witness ourself at Westminster, the eighth day of July, in the fifteenth year of our reign.

By the King: HOWARD.

The above Charter has been copied from the *Laws of the State of Rhode-Island*, published in 1822, under the superintendence of the Hon. Henry Bowen, Secretary of the State, and compared with the original. Some of the copies, in other publications, are incorrect. A persuasion that comparatively few of our citizens possess an accurate copy of this document, which is distinguished for its enlarged and enlightened principles of civil and religious freedom, and which continues still to be the fundamental law of the State, has induced its insertion in this volume.

The Charter was obtained at an auspicious moment, when Charles II., having recently ascended the throne, was not disposed to deny favors to any of his subjects. By this Charter all the powers of government were conferred upon the Colony, the King not having reserved to himself the right of revising its proceedings. At no other period, probably, could such extensive privileges have been obtained.

No. XXII.

Decision of Carr, &c., relative to Misquamacock.

We, by the power given us by his Majesty's commission, having heard the complaints of some of his Majesty's subjects, purchasers of certain lands called Misquamacock, lying on the eastern side of Pawcatuck river, and having likewise heard all the pretences of those by whom they have suffered great oppressions, and considering the grounds from whence these differences and injuries have proceeded, and endeavoring to prevent the like for the future, do declare, that no colony hath any just right to dispose of any lands, conquered from the natives, unless both the cause of that conquest be just, and the lands lie within those bonnds which the King by his charter hath given it, nor to exercise any authority beyond those bounds ; which we desire all his Majesty's subjects to take notice of for the future, lest they incur his Majesty's displeasure, and suffer a deserved punishment. We likewise declare, that all those gifts or grants of any lands, lying on the eastern side of Pawcatuck river, and a north line drawn to the Massachusetts, from the midst of the ford near to Thomas Shaw's house, and in the King's

Province, made by his Majesty's Colony of the Massachusetts, to any person whatsoever, or by that usurped authority called the United Colonies, to be void. And we hereby command all such as are therein concerned to remove themselves and their goods from the said lands, before the nine and twentieth day of September next. In the mean time, neither hindering the Pequot Indians from planting there this summer, nor those of the King's Province, who are the purchasers, from improving the same, as they will answer the contrary. Given under our hands and seals, at Warwick, April 4th. 1665.

ROBERT CARR,   [L. S.]
GEORGE CARTWRIGHT,   [L. S.]
SAMUEL MAVERICK,   [L. S.]
[Colony Records.]

No. XXIII.

Commission from Carr, &c., 1665.

Whereas, by the authority given us by his sacred Majesty, our dread Sovereign, to provide for the peace and safety of all his Colonies here in America, and in a more especial manner for that part of it called the Narragansett country, and by his Majesty commanded now to be called the King's Province: We did, by commission under our hands and seals, dated at Petaqumskocte March the twentieth 1664, appoint, authorize, and in his Majesty's name require, Benedict Arnold, William Brenton, Esquires, John Coggeshall, James Barker, Joseph Clarke, William Field, Thomas Olney, Roger Williams, William Baulston,

John Sanford, Randall Howldon, Walter Todd, John Porter and John Greene, Gntlemen, to exercise the power and authority of Justices of the peace or magistrates, throughout the whole compass of this his Majesty's Province, and to do whatsoever they think best for the peace and safety of the said Province, and as near as they can to the English laws, till his Majesty's pleasure be farther known therein; and in matters of greater consequence, any seven of them, whereof the Governor or Deputy Governor shall be one, shall be a Court to determine any business: Our intent and meaning was and is, that the said commission should be no longer in force, than until the 3d. of May next, and that then and thenceforward, the Governor and Deputy Governor, and all the Assistants for the time being of his Majesty's Colony of Rhode-Island &c. shall be Justices of the peace. And therefore by the power given us from his Majesty, we order and appoint the Governor and Deputy Governor, and all the Assistants of the said Colony, for the time being, to be and to exercise the authority of Justices of the peace in this the King's Province, and to do whatever they think best for the peace and safety of the said Province, and as near as they can to the English laws, till his Majesty's pleasure be farther known therein; and in matters of greater consequence, any seven of them, whereof the Governor or Deputy Governor shall be one, shall be a Court to determine any business.   Given under our hands and seals, at Warwick, April 8th. 1665.

  ROBERT CARR,   [L. S.]

  GEORGE CARTWRIGHT, [L. S.]

  SAMUEL MAVERICK,   [L. S.]

         [Colony Records.]

No. XXIV.—[p. 120.]

Episcopal Church.

The following account of the establishment of the Episcopal Church in Rhode-Island is taken from an historical account of the " Society for the propagation of the Gospel in Foreign Parts, by David Humphries, D. D., Secretary to the Sosiety, London, 1730."

"In September 1702, the Church-wardens of Rhode-Island, wrote to the Society, 'That they cannot forbear expressing their great joy in being under the patronage of so honorable a Corporation, through whose pious endeavors, with God's assistance, the Church of England hath so fair a prospect of flourishing in those remote parts of the world, and among the rest of her small branches, theirs also in Rhode-Island: That though it is not four years since they began to assemble themselves together to worship God after the manner of the Church of England, yet have they built them a church, finished all on the outside, and the inside is pewed well, though not beautiful; and whatsoever favors the Society shall bestow upon them towards the promoting of their Church, shall be received with the humblest gratitude, and seconded with the utmost of their abilities.' p. 61, 62.

" The Society resolved to send a Missionary hither, both on account of their being the first, and also a numerous people, settled on a flourishing Island. The Rev Mr. Honyman was appointed in 1704. He discharged the duties of his mission with great diligence. p. 318, 319. He represented also very earnestly to the Society, the want of a Missionary at a town called Providence, about thirty miles from Newport, a place very considerable for the number of its inhabitants. The Society appointed in the next year (1723) the Rev. Mr. Pigot Missionary there. Besides the faithful discharge of his duty at his own station, Mr. Honyman hath been farther instrumental in gathering several congregations at Naragansett, Tiverton, Freetown, and at the above mentioned place, Providence. p. 320, 321.

" The people of Naragansett county (North-Kingston) made application to the Bishop of London, about the year 1707, for a Missionary, and built a church soon after by the voluntary contributions of its inhabitants. In the year 1717, the Society appointed the Rev. Mr. Guy to that place; he arrived there soon after, and entered upon his mission with much zeal. He removed to South-Carolina, in 1719. The Rev. Mr. M'cSparran was appointed Missionary there in 1720. p. 324, 326.

" The chief inhabitants of Bristol, in the year 1720, wrote very earnest letters to the Bishop of London and to the Society, for a Minister of the Church of England, and promised to build a church. The Rev. Mr. Orrem was sent Missionary here in 1722. Mr. Orrem gained the esteem and affection of the people very much, and proceeded in his mission with success." p. 331, 332.

No. XXV.—[p. 126.]

Philip's War.

On the 29th of March, 1676, a large body of Indians attacked Providence and burned more than thirty houses in the north part of the town, in one of which were the town records. They were saved by being thrown into the Mooshausick; from thence they were afterwards taken, though much injured, and sent to Newport for safe keeping, where they remained during the remainder of the war.

Philip's War lasted more than a year, and was the most distressing period that New-England had ever seen, and threatened the total extirpation of her colonies. About six hundred men, the flower of her strength, fell in battle or were butchered by the savages. In Massachusetts, Plymouth and Rhode-Island, twelve or thirteen towns were utterly destroyed. About six hundred dwelling houses were burned; a heavy debt was contracted, and a vast amount of property destroyed. There were few families who did not lose some beloved relative in this calamitous war, and a general gloom spread through the country.

No. XXVI.

A list of the Presidents of the Colony of Rhode-Island and Providence Plantations, under the first Patent; and of the Governors, under the second Charter, collected from the State Records.

Presidents under the first Patent.

1647 John Coggeshall, to   1648
1648 Jeremiah Clarke, to   1649
1649 John Smith, to   1650
1650 Nicholas Easton, to   1652

In the year 1651, William Coddington went to England, and procured from the Council of State, a commission, dated April 3, 1651, constituting him Governor for life of Rhode-Island, Canonicut, &c., with which he returned about the 1st of August, of that year. This produced much uneasiness in the Colony. All the inhabitants on the main, refused to submit to Coddington's government. The Colony appointed Roger Williams and John Clarke to proceed to England, to procure the repeal of Coddington's commission. After much opposition, they effected this in 1652. Mr. Williams returned, and at a General Election, held at Warwick, on the 12th of September, 1654, was chosen President of the Colony. Dr. Clarke continued in England as the Colony's agent, till he obtained the Charter granted by Charles II. in 1663.

1654 Roger Williams, to   1657
1657 Benedict Arnold, to   1660

1660	William Brenton, to	1662
1662	Benedict Arnold, to	1663

Governors under the second Charter.

1663	Benedict Arnold, to	1666
1666	William Brenton, to	1669
1669	Benedict Arnold, to	1672
1672	Nicholas Easton, to	1674
1674	William Coddington, to	1676
1676	Walter Clarke, to	1677
1677	Benedict Arnold, to	1679
1679	John Cranston, to	1680
1680	Peleg Sanford, to	1683
1683	William Coddington, to	1685
1685	Henry Bull, to	1686
1686	Walter Clarke	
1686	The Charter superseded by Sir Edmund Andross, but restored in	
1689	Henry Bull, to	1690
1690	John Easton, to	1695
1695	Caleb Carr, to	1696
1696	Walter Clarke, to	1698
1698	Samuel Cranston, to	1727
1727	Joseph Jenckes, to	1732
1732	William Wanton, to	1734
1734	John Wanton, to	1741
1741	Richard Ward, to	1743
1743	William Greene, to	1745
1745	Gideon Wanton, to	1746
1746	William Greene, to	1747

1747 Gideon Wanton, to 1748
1748 William Greene, to 1755
1755 Stephen Hopkins, to 1757
1757 William Greene, to 1758
1758 Stephen Hopkins, to 1762
1762 Samuel Ward, to 1763
1763 Stephen Hopkins, to 1765
1765 Samuel Ward, to 1767
1767 Stephen Hopkins, to 1768
1768 Josias Lyndon, to 1769
1769 Joseph Wanton, to 1775
1775 Nicholas Cooke, to 1778
1778 William Greene, to 1786
1786 John Collins, to 1789
1789 Arthur Fenner, to 1805
1805 Henry Smith, *acting Governor* to 1806
1806 Isaac Wilbour, *lieutenant Governor* to 1807
1807 James Fenner, to 1811
1811 William Jones, to 1817
1817 Nehemiah R. Knight, to 1821
1821 William C. Gibbs, to 1824
1824 James Fenner, to 1831
1831 Lemuel H. Arnold, to 1833
1833 John Brown Francis.